learned about society from someone who spent his career working at its fringes. Anyone who cares about justice – whether citizen or politician – should read this book'

Sarah Langford, author of *In Your Defence*

'I've never heard the job described better by anyone. John Sutherland gives a unique and personal insight into what it really means to be a police officer in modern England. The adrenaline rushes, the dreadful tedium of bureaucracy, walking on eggshells for fear of offending anyone, the moments of stark horror or overwhelming sadness; the indescribable thrill of making a difference to someone's life and the depths of despair when you fail. The overwhelming workload and the emotional overload, seeing more things daily than most people will ever see in a lifetime. Running towards danger when everyone else is running away. A job that on any given day can send your spirits soaring to the heavens, or leave your soul scarred forever'

Peter James

'This is an important book, one that should be read by the Home Secretary and every member of Parliament, as well as every newspaper editor and crime correspondent. John Sutherland is someone who after twenty-five years of police experience has a remarkable story to tell... One that we ignore at our peril'

Jeffrey Archer

'John Sutherland has a more intelligent grasp of 'The Job' and its place in a troubled society than anyone I know'

Alastair Stewart

Crossing the Line

Crossing the Line

John Sutherland

WEIDENFELD & NICOLSON

First published in Great Britain in 2020 by Weidenfeld & Nicolson
This paperback edition published in 2021 by Weidenfeld & Nicolson
an imprint of The Orion Publishing Group Ltd
Carmelite House, 50 Victoria Embankment
London EC4Y 0DZ

An Hachette UK Company

1 3 5 7 9 10 8 6 4 2

A CIP catalogue record for this book is
available from the British Library.

ISBN (Paperback) 978 1 4746 1237 1
ISBN (eBook) 978 1 4746 1238 8
ISBN (Audio) 978 1 4746 1239 5

Typeset at The Spartan Press Ltd,
Lymington, Hants

Printed and bound in Great Britain by Clays Ltd,
Elcograf S.p.A.

www.weidenfeldandnicolson.co.uk
www.orionbooks.co.uk

For Jessie, Charlie and Emily

Contents

I. *Introduction – Nothing but the Truth*

I want you to see the things that I've seen.

In the kitchen of the house across the street from where you live; outside the takeaway as evening draws in; on the top deck of the bus that passes the end of your road; among the away supporters on a Saturday afternoon and in the town centre on a Saturday night; in the stairwell where teenagers gather and needles collect; on stretches of grubby pavement and in the alleyway that runs behind the shops; outside the school gates and next to the skate park; in the burned-out remains of the third-floor flat; in the heart of the woods and out in the wide-open spaces; among the urgent raised voices in A&E. In places so close and yet so far away; in the lives of those whose faces might be familiar but whose stories we do not know.

*

I was sixteen years old when I decided that I wanted to become a police officer. Later, when the careers fair came to my university, there was only one stand I visited. After graduating, there was only one application form I filled out, one interview that I went for. I had set my heart on adventure – on living a life less ordinary than the one that might have been expected of a politely spoken, reasonably well-educated middle-class boy. More than anything, I wanted to be part of something that mattered. I joined the Met at the age of twenty-two and served as an officer for more than twenty-five years. It was my duty and my joy.

As a society, we are captivated by policing – by tales of diamond heists and gruesome deaths, of shotgun-toting bank raiders and breakneck car chases, of midnight stakeouts and barefoot mavericks tackling terrorists in tower blocks. We watch police procedurals and fly-on-the-wall documentaries and we absorb the headlines on the rolling news. Both in fiction and in real life, we can find police officers almost everywhere we look: the good ones and the bad ones, the brave ones and the bent ones, the lone ones and those who muddle their way through in odd-couple partnerships, the new ones and the world-weary veterans approaching retirement – the ones who are 'too old for this shit'. They seem so familiar to us, and yet we live our lives some distance removed from the realities of the world that policing inhabits and reveals.

Blue-and-white cordon tape flicks idly in the breeze at the scene of the latest crime. It is makeshift and insubstantial, but it establishes something solid and impermeable: a line that separates police officers from the rest of us, their place from ours. We might pause for a moment to stare at the people in forensic suits fingertip-searching for clues and wonder what might have happened there, but we always move on in the end. We resume our lives, leaving them to theirs.

The painful privilege of policing is to encounter all of life and all of death and everything in between – at the scenes not just of crimes, but of car crashes and cot deaths and every other kind of catastrophe. And in those places, the job of a police officer is to save lives, to find the lost, to bind up the broken-boned and the broken-hearted, to protect the vulnerable, to defend the weak, to confront the dangerous, sometimes to risk it all. Viewed in those terms, it seems to me to be about as extraordinary a job as could ever be. If you were to ask any police officer why they do what they do, they would more than likely tell you that it is simply because they want to make a difference. They want to help people.

When I started out in the Met in the early 1990s, I knew very little of the world beyond my own immediate, limited experience. I had spent the first fifteen years of my life in a village and then a small town, both about forty miles west of London, and while my childhood was far from perfect, there was an innocence and simplicity to things. I had never seen a pub fight or a stabbing. I'd never encountered drug addiction or child sexual exploitation. I'd never witnessed a serious house fire or a major road accident. I'd never even seen a dead body. It wasn't that I was completely ignorant – I read the papers and watched the news, just like everyone else – and it wasn't that I had no interest or didn't care. I suppose that I was in the realm of Rumsfeld's unknown unknowns: I didn't know what I didn't know. But I took an oath and I put on a uniform and, over time, everything changed. I started to see life – and death – as it actually can be.

And I want you to see it too. I want you to cross the line

from one side of the cordon tape to the other and to stand for a while in the places where police officers spend their working lives.

Some of what you will find is unavoidably grim. Some of it is horrifying and some of it defies description and comprehension. But there is beauty too: kindness, courage, compassion and humanity – the very best of things alongside the very worst. Though I am retired now, I retain a deep love for policing – both for the job and for the people who do it. It remains for me as much an affair of the heart and the soul as it ever was. And it will always be so much more than just an occupation – a means of paying the rent. It is a preoccupation, a vocation, a calling even; one that offers a singular, shattering perspective on some of the most profound and troubling problems of our age.

In the pages that follow, I will set out ten particular challenges facing us in twenty-first-century Western society: alcohol abuse, drug addiction, domestic violence, knife crime, mental illness, community–police relations, public disorder, terrorism, sexual offences and child abuse – each viewed through the lens of policing experience. The intention is not to shock or sensationalise, but rather to engage and inform; to ask questions and to suggest ways in which we ought to respond. I want to show you how life can be for people who live all around us – people who, in endless different ways, are just like you and me.

Before I continue, I want to make clear that I am no blind apologist for the job I used to do. Not all of policing history makes for comfortable reading. Think of Hillsborough, or of the failures of the first police investigation into the murder of Stephen Lawrence, or the death of Ian Tomlinson during the G20 protests in London. Sometimes police officers, both individually and collectively, get things terribly wrong – and we should never seek to pretend otherwise. We also need to understand that, while the sight of a police officer will likely be a source of immediate reassurance to many of us – the relief of knowing that everything is going to be all right now that the police are here – for some, even the fleeting presence of a copper can be the cause of overwhelming anxiety. To them, the uniform represents a threat – the possibility that they will be targeted, stopped, searched, arrested, even beaten. They might have encountered any of those things in the past, or they might have heard the second-hand stories of those who have. Either way, they are afraid. Even the most law-abiding among us can sometimes feel that jab of groundless apprehension when we catch sight of a police car in our rear-view mirror. For a small minority the response goes way beyond fear. For them, the uniform becomes a target, for everything from a mouthful of gob to a bullet or a bomb. You can still find the letters ACAB tattooed onto the knuckles of some old villains: All Coppers Are Bastards. It's a question of perception, I suppose – of belief, and of experience.

Certainly society has every right to expect higher standards of police officers than they do of anyone else. Because of the promises they make, the powers they are given and the position they occupy in society. Because if you can't trust a police officer, then who can you trust? When police officers betray their promises or misuse their powers or abuse their position, it is essential that they are brought to account. We must never shy away from holding policing up to the light, and no right-thinking police officer would ever argue otherwise.

But, having acknowledged some of the uncomfortable truths about the faults and failings of our police service, we need to take care to ensure that they don't become defining. Because the fact is, at its best, policing in this country represents the very finest of who we are and the very best of who we can be. For more than twenty-five years, I worked with heroes.

One final note before we begin. During the course of my police service, I was frequently called upon to give evidence in court. Each time I did so, I was required to take an oath. I stepped into the witness box and, taking a Bible in my right hand and raising it to shoulder height, repeated the following words:

> *I swear by Almighty God that the evidence I give to the court shall be the truth, the whole truth and nothing but the truth.*

I make the same promise to you now. The content of this book represents the evidence of my experience – of all my time in policing – and, while occasional names and identifying details might have been changed, I swear that all of it is true.

II. *Drunk and Incapable*

The first person I ever arrested, way back in the spring of 1993, was a drunk. A man who had fallen out of the bottom of life.

I had just completed my first twenty weeks of recruit training at Hendon in north London and was at the start of my Street Duties course – a further ten weeks out on patrol in the company of an older, more experienced officer who would tell me to forget most of what I had learned in the classroom and show me how to do the job for real. It didn't take me long to realise that experience is everything; that you learn policing by doing it.

We were walking down Victoria Street early one evening when I came across a soiled, sorry-looking heap of a man, slumped on the pavement just outside McDonald's. He was in no fit state to look after himself but was too drunk to even care.

Victoria Street is situated in a busy part of central London, humming with tourists, office workers, shoppers, schoolchildren, street sweepers and the constant toing and froing of red buses and black cabs. It runs more or less west to east, connecting the affluence of Belgravia with the towered magnificence of Parliament Square. A road from wealth to power. Mostly, it's a place of retail and restaurants, of banking and business, of capital and consumption, but about a third of the way up, on the right-hand side – in a space between glass and grey slab blocks – is Westminster Cathedral. And in front of the cathedral there is a broad square, with a shoe shop on one side and the McDonald's on the other. It's a place where priests and parishioners mingle and people of all faiths and none pause to take out their cameras and take in the sights.

That's where I found the semi-conscious man, some distance away from the throng, unwashed for weeks and smelling of urine. His clothes, encrusted with every kind of filth, were disintegrating, his hair was matted, his face was stubbled and scarred. I had recently celebrated my twenty-third birthday; he might have been anywhere between thirty and sixty. And you learn early on in a policing career that sometimes it might be necessary to put on a pair of latex gloves before touching another human being.

I arrested him for being drunk and incapable. I did so for his own protection. Had he at some point recovered the wherewithal to stagger back to his feet, there would probably have been nothing to stop him from falling off the edge of the kerb and into the path of the next passing vehicle. He needed saving from himself. I hauled him up off the ground and half carried him on a slow, foot-dragging walk to the waiting van. I eased him onto the floor in the back of the old Leyland Sherpa and did my best to manoeuvre him into the recovery position in preparation for the short journey back to Rochester Row nick.

Police officers are considered in law to be expert witnesses when it comes to the question of drunkenness. Over time, you learn certain stock phrases that become part of your professional vocabulary:

His eyes were glazed.
He was unsteady on his feet.
His breath smelt strongly of intoxicating liquor.

That was the evidence I presented to the custody sergeant when we reached the station, anxious to make sure I got the right words in the right order. Under most circumstances, the sergeant would then have asked for the prisoner's personal details and explained to them their rights – to speak to a solicitor, to have someone informed of their arrest and to read a copy of a (very dull) book called the *Codes of Practice*, which explains police powers and procedures. But the man's condition was such that it was impossible to get a single syllable of sense out of him. Any attempts at conversation would have been a complete waste of everyone's time.

'Take him straight down to cell two, search him and then let him sleep it off.'

The sergeant had seen people like him a thousand times before. After a while, I would develop the same kind of weary familiarity. You very quickly lose count of the drunks you meet.

'And make sure you put the mattress down on the floor. I don't want him rolling off the bench and doing himself even more damage.'

Drunks like mine were put on half-hour checks – roused every thirty minutes to make sure their alcohol-induced stupor didn't deteriorate into some other kind of medical emergency. But shouting through the small wicket in the cell door isn't enough to wake a semi-comatose alcoholic, so I was taught to pinch an ear lobe or put pressure on a thumbnail by pressing firmly against it with the side of a Bic biro. It was never my intention to cause distress, just to create enough discomfort to confirm they were still alive.

Sometimes drunks would be charged and sent to court the following morning, where they would pick up a fine they couldn't afford to pay, or more likely be sentenced retrospectively to the night they had already spent in our cells. Alternatively, they would be released straight from the station – once they'd sobered up enough – and we could save a bit of time by doing a little less paperwork. Either way, they would wander out of the door to resume their lives on the streets and on the booze. Get drunk, get arrested, get released; repeat indefinitely until organ failure kicks in and life reaches its own jarring conclusion. So often it falls to police officers to take care of people that most of the rest of the world doesn't appear to give a damn about. It might only be for one night, but if not us, then who?

I have long forgotten most of the inebriates I've dealt with over the years. But every police officer remembers their first arrest, and the man outside McDonald's was mine. I imagine he died a long, long time ago, but I still think about him. I still wonder about the circumstances of his life and the end-lessly complex set of reasons why he might have ended up on that particular bit of London pavement.

Perhaps he was ex-military, a broken veteran of the Falk-lands or some other distant conflict; someone who drank to forget. Maybe he was an ex-husband who had lost his mar-riage and his children and hit the bottle in a forlorn effort to drown the despair. Or maybe it was the bottle that had cost him his family in the first place. Perhaps it all started when he lost his job, after a downturn in the economy or an accident on the building site where he worked; having lost his source of regular income, he then also lost his home and ended up on the streets, drinking to keep out the cold. Maybe he was sick, seeking relief from physical pain or suffering from some kind of mental illness and drinking for reasons he didn't really understand. Except that it had become the only way he could get himself to sleep at night. A friend of mine who is a recovering alcoholic and who now works with alcoholics serving time in prison has suggested to me that 'addiction is an attempt at self-repair' – a desperate and singularly flawed means of trying to cope when life begins to fall apart.

For the man outside McDonald's, it might have been any one of those things. Or none of them. Or some combination of them. But the one thing I am certain of is the sadness: the deep sorrow of a life lived without apparent comfort or care. Without love. Nobody chooses an existence that turns out like that: weeping sores, freezing nights, aching limbs and endless fear. And as we walk on by, hands deep in pockets, carefully ignoring the voice asking if we have any change to spare, avoiding discomfiting eye contact with the sad soul trying to communicate with us, we are in danger of forgetting their humanity, and of forfeiting some of our own.

Over the course of my years in policing, I met every possible kind of drunk. It wasn't just the street sleepers and bedsit dwellers, fighting and losing their private battles with the alcoholic disease; it was everyone else as well.

There were young drunks and old drunks. Male drunks and female drunks. Rich drunks and poor drunks: drunks from the tower blocks and drunks from the Houses of Parliament. Celebratory drunks and mourning drunks – drinking to remember, drinking to forget. Drunks riding bicycles and drunks driving cars. Agitated drunks and passed-out-cold drunks. Happy drunks and immensely violent drunks. Drunks kissing people. Drunks killing people. The Institute of Alcohol Studies estimates that alcohol is an aggravating factor in as many as a million crimes committed in the UK each year, and that the annual cost to the UK taxpayer of alcohol-related crime and disorder is as high as £11 billion.[1]

*

The first pub fight I encountered happened in one of the back streets just off Vauxhall Bridge Road in central London.

Before joining the police, I had rarely encountered significant violence of any kind. There was the odd schoolboy scuffle, and a black eye I picked up soon after I turned eighteen, but that was about it. So the sight of my first full-blown punch-up caught me unawares. I had never seen anything like it before, not in real life, at least. The scene that greeted me as I arrived bore an uncanny resemblance to the bar-room brawls staged in a thousand Westerns – bodies tumbling through swing doors and into the street outside. All we were missing were the Stetsons and the spurs. Arms swinging, blows connecting, voices screaming, people falling – and every single one of them off their face.

I followed my colleagues into the heart of the melee and tried to take hold of the nearest flailing limb. A stray hand reached out and grabbed my epaulette, ripping it clean off the shoulder of my jacket. For a fleeting moment I worried that the damage to my uniform was going to get me into trouble with my sergeant, and I wondered how I was going to mend it. But then it was back to the chaos of the brawl. Within a minute or two, we had it under control, pulling bodies apart as they continued to issue threats of recrimination. Boozed-up bravado, all for show. Mountain goats butting heads in some pathetic, primal attempt to prove who was hardest.

I've no idea what started it, but we finished it. Bloodied noses were carted off to custody. Bystanders were ushered back indoors. Broken glass was swept away. Move along now. Nothing to see here. Over time, the violence became more and more familiar to me, particularly when it came to pubs and clubs.

Several years later, I was in the front passenger seat of a marked patrol car, parked up opposite the Slug and Lettuce pub on Fulham Broadway. I had recently moved to Fulham to take up a post as an inspector on a uniform response team, and Adrian, the senior sergeant on my new team, was showing me round. It was close to midnight.

'Why are we sitting here?' I asked him, keen to continue our tour of the local area.

He nodded his head towards the pub. 'Because at some point in the next ten minutes, there's going to be a fight on the pavement outside the Slug.'

We only had to wait five. A great tree trunk of a man emerged from the pub, landed a punch that floored one of the other drinkers, then ran off in the general direction of the Tube station. We were straight out of the car and after him. As I ran, I shouted into my radio, 'Chasing suspects... Fulham Broadway towards Stamford Bridge.'

I was younger than Adrian. Fitter, too. But somehow he managed to nudge ahead of me in our pursuit. I was still on the radio, relaying the thrill of the chase. 'Right down Britannia Road. Male IC1, wearing jeans and a sweatshirt.'

Sprinting and shouting, I was gaining on him, though still not quite as quickly as Adrian.

'Right again. Moore Park Road.'

Adrian managed to get him down on the ground. I arrived a split second later, we got the handcuffs on and I arrested him for the assault. Two decades on, Adrian continues to accuse me of stealing his prisoner. I, on the other hand, insist that I had simply paced myself better and was the only one of us with enough breath left to say the words of the caution.

'Suspect detained. Can we have a van on the hurry-up, please.'

We took him back to the nick to sober up in the cells

14

before he could be interviewed and charged. Further inquiries revealed that he was a martial artist from Lithuania, wanted for rape in his home country. He was six foot six tall. I have known of cases in which a single drunk punch killed a man, and I find myself wondering what might have happened had this particular thug decided to fight us too. I for one wouldn't have stood a chance.

Everywhere I have ever worked has had its problem pubs, clubs and off-licences. They are antisocial-behaviour generators, crime generators, violence generators – all-round harm generators. People have too much to drink and have their bags and wallets and phones stolen. People have too much to drink and fall over and hurt themselves. People have too much to drink and start smashing stuff up. People have too much to drink and get into fights with one another. Or get run over. I remember one worse-for-wear man who swayed out in front of a car doing about 30 mph along one of the roads near Victoria station. He was thrown several feet in the air and a great deal further down the road. By some extraordinary miracle, he survived the double impact – first with the car and then with the road surface – but he was a mess. Even so, it's hard not to have more sympathy for the poor, traumatised, blameless car driver.

It is against the law for any member of staff in any licensed premises to serve alcohol to someone who is already drunk. But that doesn't seem to put too many of them off – not while there are huge sums of money to be made. And a drunk and his cash are easily parted.

As I progressed in my career and started to take on responsibilities that stretched across whole London boroughs, I began to seek out the venues that appeared to have the most corrosive impact on local communities – those that placed the greatest demand and strain on police resources; those that had a disproportionate impact on crime in general and violence in particular. The idea was to concentrate our attention in the locations where we were likely to get the greatest positive return on our investment of time and effort. In Hammersmith, it was the Palais.

At the lower end of Shepherds Bush Road, a hundred yards or so from the busy Broadway, the Palais was an old dance hall and concert venue that had been operating, in various guises, since the early part of the twentieth century. The Beatles and the Stones had both played there. In the late 1990s, it had been converted into a nightclub, and that was when the real problems set in. Too much drink, too many drugs and too much crime and disorder of every sort. I met with the owners and tried to work constructively with them to improve things.

Local residents had reported concerns about crowded pavements, traffic jams, litter and noise, but I had concerns far more serious than the basic inconveniences associated with having a busy nightclub on your doorstep. I was troubled by the account of the woman who reported being raped after leaving the venue; by the story of the man whose skull had been fractured in a fight; by the outbreak of violence serious enough for my colleagues to call out the Commissioner's Reserve, a specialist unit of officers trained to deal with major disorder; by the shooting that happened on the dance floor.

In early 2006, having been unable to secure any voluntary improvement in the situation, my colleagues and I initiated a formal review of the venue's licence. In doing so, I was given legal advice suggesting that I needed to consider the human rights of the Palais owners and staff – their entitlement to a livelihood and so on. But, to be honest, I was more concerned about the human rights of everyone else. We built our case on the basis of a desire to prevent crime and disorder, and to preserve public safety. Our senior crime analyst developed a comprehensive and very lengthy chronological document that set out countless cases of serious criminality and repeated instances of disorder. The hearing was held at the Town Hall, and we were successful in securing a reduction in both the venue's opening hours and its operating capacity. The case cost many thousands of pounds to bring, but the crime that had persisted for so long had cost hundreds of thousands more. A year later, the Palais closed down completely, and one little corner of the capital was a whole lot safer as a consequence.

My adversarial dealings with the Palais happened in the months following the introduction of a new set of nationwide twenty-four-hour licensing laws. They had come into effect at midnight on 24 November 2005 and had been portrayed as a solution to the so called binge-drinking epidemic that had begun to blight so many parts of the country. They certainly represented a significant shift in the regulation of alcohol sales. Rather than closing at 11 p.m. – later for some nightclubs at weekends – venues could apply for licences that would allow them to stay open, serving alcohol all the way through the night.

The idea seemed to be to encourage people to spread their drinking over an extended period of time – and to avoid the sudden rush of consumption in the period immediately prior to traditional closing times. But before the changes came into effect, there had been widespread concern expressed about the possible consequences. Medical experts highlighted the likely health costs of increased alcohol intake. Police chiefs pointed out the potential impact on crime and antisocial behaviour. And all sorts of people talked about the wider social implications of the likely emergence of a twenty-four-hour drinking culture. Some of the academic research published a decade or so later suggested that many of these fears were not borne out in reality, but experience sometimes contradicts apparent evidence.

As far as police officers are concerned, late and night shifts on Fridays and Saturdays have always been busy – particularly in town centres. But before November 2005, there were natural limitations – basic time constraints – on the kind of alcohol-related criminality and antisocial behaviour that becomes so familiar when you're out on patrol. Most places would be closed not long after midnight and the streets would be relatively quiet by about 2 a.m. At that point, we would have the precious opportunity to draw breath and perhaps even devote some time to other priorities. Not so since November 2005. From that point on, in some parts of town at least, the drinking and pissing against walls and throwing up on pavements and falling over and fighting simply carried on all the way through the night. And it placed extraordinary demands on already stretched police resources.

Take Camden Town, for example. One of the liveliest and busiest parts of central London, it is the very definition of a twenty-four-hour economy, with pubs, clubs, bars, all-night restaurants and outdoor drinking on the canal towpath, tattoo parlours and mad shops selling wigs and leopard-print clothes. People come from all over the world to visit, and among all that is genuinely wonderful about Camden, there are the all-too-evident consequences of the drinking that never stops.

I had the privilege of being the local borough commander for just over two years, between 2010 and 2012, and Camden Town was part of my patch. The relentlessly harmful impact of too much booze – specifically enabled and extended by twenty-four-hour licensing – became a source of huge concern to me. And with good reason: crime in the area was significant, violence in particular.

Sometimes it was deadly.

On Sunday 26 February 2012, Liverpool Football Club won the League Cup Final. The match was played at Wembley, and thousands of supporters had travelled down to London the night before. One of them, twenty-six-year-old Alex Jarmay, never made it to the game. He and his younger brother, together with a handful of friends, went out drinking in Camden Town, no doubt dreaming out loud about goals being scored and trophies being lifted. Scousers are pretty passionate about their football. But in a basement bar just off Camden High Street, it all went fatally wrong. Twenty-nine-year-old Paul Beck was drinking in the same bar as the group of friends. He had also been taking cocaine. Reacting to a seemingly non-existent threat, Beck crossed the dance floor and entered the venue's kitchen. I have watched the grim, silent CCTV footage of him doing so. It shows him re-emerging moments later armed with a large knife. Off camera, he stabbed Alex three times, including once in the chest. Alex staggered to the entrance of the club before collapsing and dying on the pavement outside.

The following morning, I drove up to Holborn to meet with Alex's brother and two of the friends who had been at the bar when it happened. I sat down at a table in the police station canteen and looked across at three broken men. They were silent and uncomprehending, their faces ashen and drawn: I don't think any of them had slept a single minute since the night before. I tried to find the words to tell them how deeply sorry I was, and I promised them that we would give everything in our pursuit of the killer, but I don't think they took any of it in. How could they have done? It was meant to have been a day of joy – of cup final songs and raucous celebrations – but instead, they had found themselves trapped in a waking nightmare. The words of a stranger, however sensitively spoken, could do nothing to change the reality they were faced with. Paul Beck eventually got life. Alex Jarmay lost his. And all for what? Certainly nothing that makes any kind of sense to me.

I was so concerned about the prevalence of the violence in Camden Town that, together with my senior team, I took the decision to multiply the policing presence there at weekends. On Fridays and Saturdays, in place of the usual three-shift pattern (earlies, lates and nights, each lasting eight hours), we asked officers to work two twelve-hour stretches instead. We called it Operation Numerus. Thus, the early shift became a day shift, starting at seven in the morning and finishing at seven in the evening, and all those officers who would otherwise have been working lates and nights were combined into a single team in an effort to keep a lid on things. Half of them were dedicated exclusively to Camden Town. The results were positive, but the investment of resources was disproportionate, and detrimental to other parts of the borough not blighted by the worst effects of the late-night economy, which were thus starved of a regular policing presence. That is the reality, though. You can't do more of one thing while simultaneously doing more of every other thing as well. The decision to focus attention on one particular crime problem – or on one specific geographical area – comes, inevitably, at the expense of others. It remains a constant balancing act, but one that has to be determined on the basis of harm. The greater the potential for harm to be caused, the greater the need to invest time and people and money and resources. Not everything can be a priority.

*

It seems to me that beyond the apparent desire to extend drinking hours – and in doing so somehow dilute the adverse effects of too much alcohol – the introduction of twenty-four-hour licensing was driven by two other motivations. The first might be described as libertarian and aspirational – the ambition of creating a European-style café culture that would bring new life to the kinds of inner-city areas that never really slept. The problem was that while the changes introduced a new set of drinking rights, there was no commensurate sense of accompanying responsibility demonstrated either by individual drinkers or by the licensing trade. Certainly not in places like Camden Town.

The second driver was hard-nosed economics. Successful venues were able to earn fortunes from the extended hours. But while the profits were privatised, the accompanying costs – of cleaning up streets, breaking up fights and treating those who got sick or hurt – were paid for almost entirely out of the public purse. An evidence review carried out by Public Health England in 2016 suggested that the total cost of alcohol-related harm (an estimate of the combined financial burden borne by the police, the criminal justice system, the NHS and the wider UK economy) could be as high as £52 billion every single year.[2]

Drinking too much is costing us a fortune. More than that, it is killing us. The abuse of alcohol destroys lives. It can do so as the result of a single night out or as the consequence of years of sustained drinking.

When I was working as a detective sergeant in Lewisham, I took on responsibility for investigating a rape case involving two alcoholics. They knew one other and both were known to the police. After another long day's drinking, they had ended up in bed together back at his place. No one was disputing the sex that had followed; the point of disagreement – and the basis of the allegation – was one of consent.

At some point along the way, she told us that she had said no but that he had paid no heed. And no must always mean no.

I went with a couple of members of my team to the scene of the alleged crime – a grim first-floor bedsit in which none of the limited contents, carpets or sparse furnishings appeared to have been cleaned or washed at any point in living memory. It was one of those places where you might have felt more inclined to wipe your feet on the way out rather than on the way in. The suspect was at home and we informed him of the allegation before arresting him. He told us that the sex had been consensual, but in truth, he couldn't remember much of anything at all. He was a crumbling old boozer who had likely been drinking since before I was born.

We did the job we were there to do – seizing and packaging the impossibly grubby bedclothes, along with anything else that might have been of evidential value. Then we took him down to the station. Once he was sober enough, we took a series of intimate swabs and samples from him, before sitting him down in a tape-recorded interview room and asking him to tell us what had happened. He suggested that they had been drinking together – as they often did – and that she had been a perfectly willing participant in all that followed. His rambling account was peppered with the sort of nose-wrinkling detail that is hard to shift from the imagination, even two decades later.

While we were dealing with him, one of the DCs on my team – a specially trained SOIT (Sexual Offences Investigation Techniques) officer – was attending to the victim. Murder aside, rape is about as wicked a crime as it's possible to commit, and those who have been attacked need and deserve every possible consideration and care. The officer accompanied the victim to the nearest Haven clinic – a bespoke medical facility for victims of rape and sexual assault – but once there, she was reluctant to submit to the doctor's examination or to provide the evidential samples that were essential for the investigation. She maintained that she had been raped, but was unwilling to elaborate much further or to give any kind of written statement. I suspect that hers was a life so chaotic that this turn of events was just the latest in a seemingly endless procession of sadness. And now she just wanted to be left alone.

All of which meant that we were stuck. Rape cases always require patience, and in this instance, we had no option but to release the suspect on police bail while we tried to progress our inquiries.

He went back to the drink, she went back to the drink, and I never managed to get any further with the allegation. I tried visiting her at home and found her standing on the pavement just outside her flat. I offered my support and promised her that we would take the matter seriously if only she would give us a statement. But she was having none of it. The SOIT officer had been similarly unsuccessful on every occasion she had tried to speak to her. Reluctantly, I closed the file. She was a complete mess – the victim not just of an alleged rape, but of life itself. As with the man I arrested outside McDonald's, I find myself wondering at her story – at the particular collection of circumstances and events that had left her that way. The man who might or might not have raped her was a complete mess too. Two shambolic lives entirely destroyed by alcohol, leaving us with a truth that would never be known.

*

In 2018, the Scottish government introduced new legislation to set minimum unit pricing levels for alcohol. The primary source of their concern was the sort of cheap booze that often fills the lower shelves in local off-licences – the extra-strength beer and cider and the own-brand spirits that seem to be consumed almost exclusively by problem drinkers: kids with pocket money and mischief in mind and adults long since lost to the demon drink. Availability and affordability were the twin roots of the problem. The government's aim was a simple one: to reduce crime and disorder and save lives by lowering the amount that people drink. The tactics were straightforward too: raise the price of alcohol to the point where it becomes far less affordable to the young and those who abuse it.

Prior to the introduction of minimum pricing, it was possible to buy a three-litre bottle of strong cider for less than £4. Such a bottle contains twenty-two units of alcohol – significantly higher than the Chief Medical Officer's recommended limit of fourteen units for an adult to consume in an entire week. Similarly, it was possible to buy a 75 cl bottle of own-brand vodka for £10. One of those contains closer to twenty-eight units of alcohol.

Those lower prices are still available in England, Wales and Northern Ireland, though the latter two countries have taken some steps towards the introduction of minimum unit pricing. But in Scotland, the minimum price has been set at 50p per unit, meaning that the cost of the bottle of cider has risen to £11 and the vodka to £14. If that seems like an enormous price hike, a 2018 BBC News report estimated that annual alcohol-related health and criminal justice expenditure in Scotland is somewhere in the region of £3.6 billion. And the human cost is greater still. There are twenty-two alcohol-specific deaths in Scotland every single week. There are also 697 alcohol-related hospital admissions each week, and 80 per cent of all assault victims seen in A&E departments have been drinking.[3]

Time will tell whether the new laws work as they are intended to, but every instinct I have tells me that it's the right thing to do. And that the rest of Britain should do likewise. It won't be the answer to everything, but it will be an almighty step in the right direction.

*

As I look back over my service, I cannot think of a single circumstance or situation I encountered in which alcohol made things better. In fact, exactly the opposite is true. Alcohol is both an enabling and an aggravating factor in endless forms of criminality – domestic violence (indeed, violence of almost every kind), sexual assault and harassment, child sexual exploitation and so on. And then there are the roads. In Britain in 2017, there were more than 8,500 casualties following drink-driving accidents, including 290 fatalities and 1,400 serious injuries.[4]

As F. Scott Fitzgerald wrote in *The Great Gatsby*: 'First you take a drink, then the drink takes a drink, then the drink takes you.' Extend that over the course of an evening and into the early hours of the following morning, and you have the potential for every possible kind of trouble. Extend it over the course of a lifetime, and you will likely find yourself in the arms of a police officer, being peeled off the pavement outside a fast-food restaurant in the centre of town.

If alcohol was a twenty-first-century discovery, it would be designated as a Class A drug, no different from heroin or cocaine. As the law currently stands, it would be illegal to sell it. It would be illegal even to possess it.

III. *Possession with Intent*

Brixton in the 1990s was a remarkable place to work as a police officer: there was so much that needed doing, with barely a breath between one incident and the next, and always a difference to be made in the life of somebody, somewhere. It was the second posting of my Met career. I had started out as a PC in a much quieter part of town and was looking for a new professional challenge. I wanted to learn and develop – to experience everything that a life in blue had to offer. So I was delighted when my request for a move south of the river was approved.

One afternoon, I was asked to help out on a response team that was short of an officer for the late shift. I was posted as the operator in a marked patrol car being driven by an older, more experienced PC called James Seymour. I hadn't met him before, but he turned out to be extraordinary company. Part way through the evening, in a brief lull between calls, he told me the story of the day he nearly died.

It all happened on the night of Wednesday 9 March 1994.

It was a late turn much like any other, and PC 965LD Seymour was driving Lima 3, one of the division's area cars, tasked with responding to the most serious emergency calls. His operator was a young colleague from the same response team. It was approaching 9.30 p.m. – close to the end of the shift – and the two officers were patrolling 'the Frontline', a neighbourhood synonymous with street-level drug dealing on an almost industrial scale.

As they drove down Atlantic Road towards the centre of Brixton, the traffic was stationary up ahead. They watched as a high-powered motorcycle with pillion passenger on board went straight through the red light at the next junction and turned left into Coldharbour Lane. The officers weren't close enough to get the number plate or any meaningful description of the two people, and there seemed no sense in turning on the blues and twos straight away. It might have been nothing, and in any case, cars are no match for motorbikes in the event of a chase through crowded inner London streets. So they bided their time.

As the lights changed, Lima 3 made a slow left turn into Coldharbour Lane, passing a pub called the Atlantic on the left-hand side. A short distance up the road, the officers spotted two men in crash helmets walking along the pavement in the general direction of the pub. Their body language just wasn't right. They seemed startled by the presence of the police car, coming to a sudden stop as it passed them. James reacted by taking the next turning on his left, into Rushcroft Road. There, immediately in front of them, was the motorbike, sitting unattended on the far side of the street. They ran a quick check on the number plate and it came back as having no current keeper. Why would the owner of an expensive bike not want it registered with the authorities?

James drove round the block and came back down Coldharbour Lane in the opposite direction, with Rushcroft Road and the Atlantic now on their right. A couple of minutes had gone by since their first sighting of the two men, but now they spotted them again, this time inside a chicken shop.

Police officers looking at suspects looking at police officers.

James turned the car round at the first opportunity and headed straight back to the takeaway. In the intervening moments, the suspects had left, but as Lima 3 arrived in Rushcroft Road for the second time, there they were, standing right next to the bike. James pulled up alongside them, pulse quickening a little, and he and his operator got out to talk to them. He explained what they had seen and told them that they were both going to be searched for drugs. As they had been trained to do, the officers separated the two men and walked them a short distance apart from one another – just far enough to ensure they couldn't communicate and concoct some shared work of fiction to explain their presence in the neighbourhood. Again, as they had been taught, the PCs kept one another in full view at all times. It was a textbook stop.

Then, without warning, the atmosphere changed. The particular street sense that police officers develop after years out on patrol told James that something was very, very wrong.

He saw his suspect throw something that looked like rocks

of crack cocaine onto the ground. He responded by pushing the man firmly against the wall and reaching down in an attempt to retrieve the drugs. Out of the corner of his eye, he saw that his colleague had begun struggling with the second suspect, though the PC seemed to be gaining the upper hand. James reached for his radio to call for assistance, but he didn't get there in time. Suddenly, the second man was holding a black handgun. Perhaps it had come from the waistband of his trousers, James couldn't be sure. His whole body was surging with adrenalin now.

Then he heard a gunshot, and the sound of his colleague screaming. He saw him sprawled on the ground, reaching for his leg, seriously wounded. And, as in fiction, so in fact, everything started to slow down. This isn't happening, he said to himself.

The gunman looked straight at him and yelled, 'Fuck off.' For a fleeting moment, James didn't move. The suspect screamed at him a second time. 'Fuck off!'

It was forceful. Urgent, desperate. And then he fired three more rounds. The first two missed, but as James turned to look for cover, the third hit him in his back. The bullet passed through him like a white-hot needle, within a centimetre of his spine, grazing the top of his kidney before exiting his side. But the searing physical pain was not the most overwhelming thing. It was the mental anguish – the sense of utter helplessness.

As he lay in the road, next to a parked white van, wanting desperately to get to his injured colleague but knowing he couldn't move, he told himself very simply: I'm not going to die here. He reached round to his lower back, feeling his ripped clothing and his ripped body. He looked at his hand and saw the blood. Then he calmly placed three of his fingers into his own wound in an attempt to stem the flow. With his other hand, he reached for his radio.

'Urgent assistance... Shots fired... We've been shot...'

The suspect fired an apparent victory round into the air – they heard it over the open radio channel in the Brixton control room – before he and his accomplice got on the bike and made their escape. James felt a strange sense of relief that they would be gone before help arrived. At least it meant no one else was going to get hit.

Every available officer for miles around dropped what they were doing and responded instantaneously. Late-turn officers abandoned paperwork and every other call. Night-duty officers, newly arrived at work and still getting changed in the locker rooms, turned out in half blues, grabbing whatever kit they could in the headlong rush to get there in time. If the call is to officers down, nothing else matters more.

James began shivering as he heard the sound of the approaching sirens. No one had stopped to help them – one or two people had actually crossed the road and walked on by – but the cavalry were on their way. The first officer to arrive was one of his best mates; they were like brothers. He gave James a quick check over – 'You're all right... you're breathing' – before going straight to the second injured officer, who was by now unconscious.

James somehow managed to stay awake, and was accompanied on the journey to King's College Hospital by a PC who talked to him incessantly. He was taken straight into surgery. He remained in hospital for the next four days and was off work for six months.

Remarkably, both officers eventually made a full physical recovery. They were offered a fresh start, with a free choice of posting anywhere in London. But both asked to return to Brixton. James told me that he would have spent the rest of his life wondering what might have been had he not gone back. He just wanted to get behind the wheel of Lima 3 again and prove (to himself as much as to anyone else) that he could still do the job he loved.

The two suspects stood trial at the Old Bailey in March 1995. It was revealed that they had been going to the Atlantic that night to collect a drugs debt. They were tooled up in case of trouble. The gunman was convicted, and as he was being led away to begin his sentence, he turned and faced James across the courtroom. With the fingers of his right hand, he made the shape of a gun, and pointing them directly at the officer, he fired one last shot.

Twenty-four years after it happened, retired PC James Seymour and I sat down in a south London pub less than half a mile from Rushcroft Road and, over a pint, he remembered it all over again. There were tears in his eyes and his hands were shaking as he relived every last detail. His body might have mended, but some scars take longer to heal. He is an incredibly brave man, one who represents all that is most extraordinary about the men and women I served alongside for so many years.

*

The thing about drugs is that it can never be 'just a bit of puff' or 'just a bit of blow', even for those who might describe themselves as occasional, social users. For as long as it remains illegal to possess them in this country, the drugs that people are taking – cannabis, cocaine, Ecstasy or whatever – will in almost every case have passed at some point through the hands of men of unimaginable violence who care nothing for the lives of others.

It's never just 'a bit of personal'. That bag of weed or that paper fold of cocaine represents the final link in a long supply chain that likely stretches all the way back to Afghanistan, Colombia or some other distant place. And at every point in that chain, you will find crime in its most dreadful forms: murder, kidnap, torture, human trafficking, rape, and so the list goes on. Second only to hard cash, fear is the currency of the streets: the most successful dealers are the most terrifying ones. And unchecked greed drives unchecked violence.

At the foot of the supply chain, you find the addicts. While suppliers and dealers are responsible for staggering levels of violence and harm, some addicts create their own particular tsunami of criminality – mostly of the acquisitive kind. Of course, there are plenty of users who don't turn to other forms of offending in order to finance their habits, but figures published by the National Police Chiefs Council (NPCC) suggest that 45 per cent of all acquisitive crime – from burglary to robbery, shoplifting to car crime – is committed by regular heroin and crack users.[5] In many cases, their offending extends to stealing from members of their own families.

A former colleague of mine – a serving officer with extensive experience of undercover drugs work – talks about the 'socio-familial harm' done by drugs, by which he means the damage done to the closest relationships we experience in our lives: 'Mothers, particularly, watch their offspring become lying, cheating, manipulating thieves – a change in character that is mirrored by the often appalling physical change in their sons and daughters. The realisation that their child has become someone they cannot trust is not an overnight sensation. It is a long, drawn-out, painful and ultimately devastating journey.'

As a young PC, learning for the first time about drug-related crime, I noticed the addicts long before I noticed the dealers. Even with a minimum of operational policing experience, it was not difficult to pick them out in a crowd, with their sallow skin and sunken eyes, missing teeth, blackened gums, shuffling gait, and the kind of twitchy anxiety that offered a reasonable indication of the time that had passed since their last fix. They were some of the saddest people I ever met. Like the Brixton girl who was on the gear and on the game, selling herself to any fiend willing to pay for her next rock of crack. Like the Merton man standing a few yards away from me with a used hypodermic sticking out of the side of his own neck. Alive, but hardly living.

The world labelled them according to their drug of choice – dope-head, coke-head, crack-head, smack-head – but mostly we just called them junkies. It's a horrible expression, but one I used for years without giving it a second thought. I failed to understand just how dehumanising a single word can be – defining a person entirely according to their addiction, leaving room for nothing else besides. Whether we meant it to or not, the use of the term made them a little less than the rest of us; junkies are easy to despise.

What is it that transforms people into drug-shattered shells of themselves? For some, perhaps, the descent begins with nothing more than simple curiosity; with the irresponsible experimentation of youth. For others, there is the undeniable pleasure of the first few highs, leading to a lifetime spent in search of the next, greater one. But in a distressingly large majority of cases, taking drugs is simply a hopeless attempt to numb the pain – of violence, of abuse, of abandonment, of homelessness, of unemployment. Another former colleague of mine with a deep understanding of the subject has suggested to me that perhaps as many as two-thirds of problematic heroin users in this country are self-medicating as a means of trying to deal with the consequences of childhood trauma.[6] These are not feckless, reckless human beings, relentlessly consumed with the destruction of life. These are broken and hurting people, struggling with unimaginable torment and distress. There is no semblance of pleasure in the narcotic hit; it is just a question of surviving from one fix to the next. Theirs is medicine that kills.

As I progressed through my policing career, it wasn't just the stereotypical addicts I encountered: the middle-aged men and women with faces ridged and rutted like peach stones, to whom the years had been so very unkind. It was the unexpected ones too.

Simon Dunn was in his early twenties. He came from an

upper-middle-class family who lived in a large, comfortable home surrounded by the green fields of Dorset. Materially speaking, he had everything a young man might wish for. But something had gone terribly wrong somewhere along the line, and he became addicted to crack cocaine. In time, he exhausted all his funds and ended up in debt to his two London dealers. The streets are entirely unforgiving in such circumstances, and so, inevitably, the dealers came after him.

I sat for hours, watching and rewatching the footage of the chase – piecing together clips from several different CCTV cameras to complete a compelling real-life story of a terror-stricken man running for his life. There he was, sprinting down the street and into the hoped-for sanctuary of the railway station. There they were, less than five seconds behind him and gaining all the time. There he was, running through the ticket hall and down the stairs leading to the southbound platform. There they were, only a handful of strides behind him. There he was, jumping off the platform onto the tracks, far more terrified of them than he was of the very real prospect of being hit by a train. There they were, remorseless and relentless in their pursuit. They caught him somewhere down the tracks – somewhere off camera – and held him hostage in a flat until his debts were paid.

It was his parents who contacted the police. They were, quite understandably, at their wits' end. They invited me down to their family home, where I met Simon for the first time. He was physically safe, but he was clearly in a bad way – as a consequence of both his recent ordeal and his long-term addiction. His mum and dad weren't doing too well either. I tried to support and reassure them all, and to assist Simon in searching through his narcotic-fogged memory to recall an accurate, truthful version of what happened that day. But the only facts I could be certain of were those I had been able to establish for myself – those I had seen with my own eyes on the CCTV footage. Everything else was hazy at best. He didn't seem to know what he really knew – or he had made some kind of subconscious choice not to reveal it. When we got to the trial, the evidence against the suspects – of both kidnapping and false imprisonment – was overwhelming, but they got away with their crimes because Simon was as chaotic in the witness box as he was in life. And that left enough doubt in the minds of the jury for them to acquit. I have no idea what happened to him after he walked out of the courtroom that day. But, like so many others I encountered along the way, I have never forgotten him. A crack-ravaged ruin of a life.

*

The street dealers are the second link in the drugs supply chain – one step up from the users. Some of them are addicts too; selling gear in order to buy gear. Some of them have been coerced into selling drugs on behalf of others. But many of them are just opportunists, taking advantage of the addicts to keep themselves in gear of the non-narcotic kind – trainers, phones, bling. It's easy money and they really don't seem to care who they damage or place in harm's way as a consequence.

Those I encountered plied their trade with varying levels of sophistication. At the low-tech end, there was the Brixton man seen offering to sell cannabis resin to a passer-by. We stopped and searched him and recovered a small matchbox containing what turned out to be several cut-up pieces of liquorice that he was selling as hash. In a similar case, another suspect was found in possession of fragments of Polo mint that he was attempting to sell as crack. Offering to sell fake gear is as much a crime as supplying the real stuff.

Most dealers operated in groups that had their own informal hierarchies, each forming a link in the supply chain. In my time, I came across the 'olders', the 'youngers' and the 'tinies'.

The olders were the ones in charge of the local market – rarely touching the drugs themselves, but directing the activities of those who were carrying and serving up. ('Older' was actually something of a misnomer, since in most cases, the young men to whom the label was applied were barely out of their teens.) The youngers were the ten- to eighteen-year-olds who operated as spotters, couriers and dealers, frequently running the risk of being stopped by the police and found in possession of enough drugs to limit the likelihood of their ever being able to get away with the 'personal use' defence. But they were expendable to those who ran them. Often, they were also the ones carrying weapons, frequently out of fear, sometimes on behalf of others, often with self-defence in mind, and on occasions with undeniable murderous intent. To the extent that London's enduring knife crime problem has ever had anything to do with gangs, it was always these boys who concerned me the most.

After the youngers came the tinies – children under the

age of ten and, consequently, beneath the age of criminal responsibility. They were used to transport drugs and knives, and the chances of them being stopped by the police were almost non-existent. Even if they were caught, the stash or blade might be confiscated by the searching officers, but there would be nothing more the police could do. Just another example of the conscious and unchecked exploitation of the vulnerable in the pursuit of a foul trade and the extraordinary wealth it can bring.

Some dealers operated from flats on local housing estates. Theirs were the front doors protected by secure metal cages bolted to the brickwork, designed to frustrate the police or rival dealers intent on stealing their supplies. Punters pushed cash through the letter box and the drugs were passed back in the other direction. On the occasions when we were successful in obtaining search warrants for these places, we would have to call on the assistance of the Met's specialist 'method of entry' team. Known to all of us as 'Ghostbusters', they would turn up with an assortment of hydraulic devices, crowbars and anything else that might help them defeat the crude but robust security systems the criminals had installed, the challenge being to get through the door before the dealer flushed the gear down the toilet. As an added insurance policy, we would always put an officer or two out at the back of the premises while we were trying to get in at the front, to catch any suspects (or evidence) making a hasty exit through the rear windows.

During one search of a suspect's address, my team was joined by a specialist drugs dog and its handler. I followed them upstairs, and as we went into a young child's bedroom, the dog stopped suddenly and indicated. The source of his keen interest was a teddy bear lying in a pile of kids' clothes and toys. I picked the bear up and, turning it over, noticed that there were some threads loose in the seam that ran down its back. When I pulled them gently apart, I found a large ball of crack concealed inside the stuffing. I knew of another local drug dealer in the same neighbourhood who used to hide her stash in a pram, beneath the body of her sleeping baby.

Some dealers targeted and took advantage of their vulnerable neighbours. I recall one estate in west London that was home to a handful of residents living in supported accommodation. They had been assessed by Social Services as capable of living independently, but they were easy prey for dealers, who simply moved in and took over their lives. In doing so, they turned a safe space into a needle-ridden drugs den, and pushed some of the most defenceless people in society just a little bit closer to the edge. These days, people call it 'cuckooing'. Back then, we didn't have a name for it; we just knew that we needed to do something about it. It took a combination of concerned and courageous neighbours, switched-on housing officers and local police officers who knew their powers to provide any kind of respite. As often as not, though, the dealers got away, the addicts got another fine for possession and all of them moved on to the next flat occupied by another innocent who didn't have the capacity to say no.

Some dealers carried drugs in their mouths, serving up cling-film-wrapped rocks one spit at a time. Or they used female intermediaries to 'kiss' male clients – passing drugs from mouth to mouth without any obvious visible evidence of the transaction having taken place. They figured that by carrying the drugs in their mouths, they would be less likely to be caught in the act. And in the event that they were stopped by the police, they always had the option of swallowing the evidence. The problem was that on occasions, the drugs would get trapped in their throats and they would choke to death. Or the swallowed packaging would rupture in their stomachs, subjecting them to an unintended and fatal overdose.

In a time before mobiles, some dealers ran their businesses from local phone boxes. If they weren't there in person, you might have been able to find a number for them among the prostitution cards wallpapering the kiosk. But the advent of new technology revolutionised the drugs trade, much in the same way that it has done every other trade. The term 'county lines' is a reference to the mobile phone lines that carry tens of thousands of pounds' worth of business to provincial towns every day. The NPCC estimate that county lines are being operated in 88 per cent of all police force areas in England and Wales. Eighty-five per cent of police forces have reported that county lines groups use knives, and 74 per cent have reported the use of firearms. Sixty-five per cent of forces have reported the exploitation of children by county lines groups, in the form of human trafficking, child sexual exploitation and the coercion of young people to act as drug runners.[7] Beyond the phones, the Silk Road market on the dark web demonstrated what was possible using computers.

Methods might change, but the underlying story and the unending harm remain the same.

*

At the top of the dealing chain are the suppliers and the traffickers. These are the deadliest criminals: men of overwhelming violence who will stop at nothing to protect and advance their trade. Research presented by the NPCC suggested that drugs were a significant factor in roughly half the increase in homicides that occurred between 2014/15 and 2016/17.[8]

Early in my time as borough commander at Southwark, a known drug trafficker was killed. At his funeral, members of a rival gang turned up and attempted to murder one of the mourners, an associate of the dead man. Gunshots were fired at the graveside in the local public cemetery – like something from the fiction of the Wild West, rather than the reality of south-east London. On another occasion, I was told about a drug dealer who had been kidnapped by a rival and tortured using a searingly hot iron. And another who had cigarettes stubbed out all over his body. And another who had his testicles wired up to the mains. These are heinous crimes that are rarely reported, the terrified victims having as much to fear from the police as the suspects do. So it goes on, almost entirely hidden from the view of most of us, at least until a body turns up.

To the traffickers, it's not just drugs that are a commodity, but people too. As a young officer, I was raised on stories of mules who swallowed condoms full of cocaine and boarded international flights. Sometimes they made it through customs; sometimes they didn't. Sometimes they lived; sometimes they didn't. It was just business. In one case that defies comprehension, the drugs were stitched into the body of a recently deceased baby and carried onto a plane. The courier might have got away with it if the alarm hadn't been raised by a fellow passenger concerned that the baby hadn't made a sound for the entire duration of the long-haul flight. In this country, trafficked modern slaves are used to run cannabis factories, living and sleeping in fear and squalor while the gangmasters pile up shoeboxes full of cash.

But to me, at least, the worst traffickers of all are the bent coppers – some retired, some still serving – using their position and knowledge as cover for the betrayal of everything that every good police officer has always stood for. In the pay of organised criminal gangs or operating in small teams of their own corrupt design, they facilitate large-scale importation and onward delivery, or they seize drugs from established dealers and set up their own supply chains. In my direct experience, there aren't a significant number of them, but they are out there, and they belong in jail.

While I was still a PC at Brixton, I was offered the opportunity of a two-week attachment with the South East Regional Crime Squad (SERCS). The regional crime squads (since disbanded) had been set up to deal with criminality that crossed international borders and local force boundaries. They went after the big fish, which invariably meant they were operating at, or very close to, the top of the drugs supply chain, employing the science of sophisticated technical surveillance as well as the old-fashioned art of sitting and watching and waiting.

I spent much of that fortnight in the company of a middle-aged detective sergeant. He was the one driving the undercover car at 130 mph round the M25 and, later, showing me the set-up inside the back of one of the surveillance vehicles, fully equipped and decked out to give it the appearance of being an ordinary electrician's van. He was the one explaining the details of the current operations he was overseeing and allocating me simple administrative and investigative tasks in keeping with my lack of knowledge and experience. Three or four months after my attachment came to an end, he was the one being arrested by anti-corruption investigators. It turned out that he was bent to the core. In the few days I had spent in his company, I hadn't seen or heard a single thing that caused me any kind of concern: nothing that had looked or sounded out of place.

All the while, the good police officers – the overwhelming majority – keep doing the best they can. Because drugs don't just destroy individual lives, they cause untold damage to entire communities. Wherever I worked in London, there were always particular local neighbourhoods that were blighted by the trade, the lives and homes of ordinary, decent people overshadowed by the violent, predatory criminality of the few. In each of those places, we would put together huge policing operations, involving weeks of planning and hundreds of officers, designed to take out the dealers and reclaim the streets for their residents.

In Camden, we ran Operation Home Run, targeting drug dealers working in and around the Queens Crescent Estate, an area notorious for the violence associated with the drugs trade. We deployed undercover officers into the area to buy drugs and built up enough evidence over the course of a number of weeks to take out all the main dealers. On the appointed day, hundreds of police officers surrounded the estate and, on a signal, moved in as one to catch them all. Local people came out of their homes and applauded us as we led the suspects away. It appeared that the operation had been a huge success – a number of the officers involved were later commended by a Crown Court judge for their part in it. For a while at least, it meant that we were able to give a neighbourhood back to the silent, law-abiding majority who lived and worked there.

It was the same in Southwark. Two or three weeks into my time in charge there, there was a knock on my office door. It was the detective sergeant from the borough crime squad, and he had a bit of news for me:

'Guv'nor, we've had a few tonnes in ...'

I grinned at him and, eager to hear more, waved him into the room. These were some of my favourite moments as an operational officer – the days when everything had gone right and there was a remarkable tale to be told. I settled back in my chair to listen to what he had to say.

Because I was so new in post, I was still getting up to speed with everything that was happening on the borough. Unbeknown to me, the DS and his team had been working with officers from the National Crime Agency (NCA) on a long-running covert drugs operation, with everything coming together brilliantly that morning. They had made a series of significant arrests and had recovered, quite literally, tonnes of cocaine and cannabis, with a street value that would be counted in the millions of pounds. It was, by any measure, a spectacular result. As he came to the end of his story and left me to rejoin his team down in the custody suite, I couldn't help feeling a sense of enormous pride – in the men and women I was working with and in the results they were producing every single day.

*

Looking back now, I'm still proud of that Southwark crime squad – and of every other policing team on the borough. I'm proud to have been their boss and to have celebrated their successes. They were a bunch of brilliant people fighting the good fight with everything they had. And sometimes it even looked as though they might be winning. Except that, when it came to drugs at least, they weren't. None of us were.

Huge seizures and large numbers of arrests might slow local markets for a day or two – occasionally even for a week or two – but that was about all. Even after the most successful raids that I was involved in during my career, new drugs and new dealers quickly filled the empty spaces we had created, and the harm went unchecked in any kind of permanent sense. The basic laws of supply and demand defeated us every single time.

Politicians started talking about the 'War on Drugs' as long ago as the 1960s, and we've been losing it ever since.

In 1971, there were just over a thousand registered heroin users in the UK, and that number was falling. The drug was available to them lawfully, on prescription, and addiction was treated as a medical condition. As a consequence, there was no criminal market for heroin and no financial incentive to develop one. Addicts were patients to be supported back to full health. But 1971 was the year that saw the introduction in England and Wales of the Misuse of Drugs Act, and with it, the widespread criminalisation of drugs possession and supply. In many senses, the legislation was a political response to an emerging moral concern – apparent in some quarters at least – at the legitimised consumption of substances that were known to be harmful. Surely civil society ought to be taking a stand against that sort of thing.

In the years that followed, law enforcement agencies seized record amounts of drugs and arrested tens of thousands of users and dealers, filling the prisons in the process. And what were the consequences? By the mid-1990s, there had been little if any discernible impact on the drugs trade, but the number of heroin users in the UK had risen from 1,000 to 350,000 in the space of just two decades. The supply chain had passed into the hands of organised criminals who had every incentive to grow their client base – the greater the number of users, the greater the scale of their profits. A carefully regulated medical market became an unregulated criminal market, and people began dying in their thousands. And it wasn't just heroin, of course. Figures quoted by the NPCC estimate, for example, that the number of crack cocaine users in England alone increased from 167,000 to 183,000 between 2011/12 and 2014/15.[9]

According to the Office for National Statistics, in 2017 there were 3,756 drugs-related deaths recorded in the UK. This was the highest number since records began, and if anything (owing to local variations in the way coroners record causes of death), it was an underestimate. It was also by far the highest number of any country in Europe, accounting for one-third of the entire European total. By way of comparison, during the same period, Portugal had sixteen deaths. How can the situation be so dreadful here and, relatively speaking, so much better there?

The answer, in part at least, is that in 2001, Portugal decriminalised the possession of all drugs for personal use. Users were no longer treated as criminals, and the emphasis was instead placed on diversion and treatment for addiction. Drug addiction is now regarded as a medical issue, and the approach appears to be saving lives. It certainly appears to be working better than anything we're attempting to do in this country.

It is worth noting here that decriminalisation is not the same thing as legalisation. In the case of Portugal, the drugs themselves are still illegal, but the law enforcement effort is now concentrated on the dealers and suppliers – the people who cause the greatest harm. Legalisation would be another step entirely, and the suggestion that it should be lawful to possess and supply drugs like heroin and cocaine is an enormously controversial one.

Proponents of legalisation argue for something called a 'regulated market' – a drugs supply system that is organised and administered by government. The level and nature of regulation would vary according to drug type, and the most dangerous substances of all would remain illegal (for the same reasons that it is no longer possible to purchase 70 per cent proof rum in this country). A number of anticipated benefits are set out in support of the regulated market idea. Firstly is the notion that legalisation would take the drugs supply market out of the hands of organised crime and place it back in the hands of the state. This would have an immediate positive impact not just in terms of crippling the criminal trade, but also in terms of the endless forms of harm associated directly with its continuation. Secondly, the government would be able to raise tax revenue from legitimate supply that could then be reinvested in prevention and treatment. It is estimated, for example, that the current UK criminal market for cannabis alone is worth something like £2.5 billion every year. Thirdly, it is argued that state involvement would ensure a level of quality control in the production and supply chain that is entirely non-existent in the criminal market. Almost all MDMA deaths in this country, for example, are caused not by the drug, but by unsafe production methods and unsafe dosages.

Fourthly, legalisation would greatly reduce the burden on our enormously stretched criminal justice system. Police officers would no longer have to spend a disproportionate amount of their time dealing with low-level drugs possession cases; addicts would no longer have to steal to feed their habit, with significant knock-on benefits for acquisitive crime levels; the Crown Prosecution Service and the courts would be able to concentrate their limited resources on other priorities; and our overrun prison system might just be able to come up for air. More importantly still, an emerging generation of young people would avoid the prospect of receiving a criminal record for minor offences, with all the overwhelming life disadvantages that such a record brings. But perhaps most significantly of all, drug users themselves would be able to step out from the shadows and access the medical help and support they need to deal with their addiction.

In his book *Good Cop, Bad War*, retired undercover drugs officer Neil Woods wrote: 'We need to take a moment and just consider the possibility of not confronting the issue of drugs as a war. Legalise and regulate the supply of narcotics and at a stroke, you deprive the most vicious gangsters in the world of the £375 billion annual income that enables their operations. At a stroke, you allow some of the most vulnerable people in society to seek help for their addictions, instead of being shoved into prison cells. And, at a stroke, you allow the police to get back to doing the vitally important work they are actually trained to do...'

In 2018, Canada introduced a regulated market for cannabis, meaning that it is now legal to possess the drug for personal use and even to grow a limited number of plants at home. The government controls pricing, with the intention of making the drug available at a cost that undercuts any possible criminal market. State involvement should also allow for the regulation of harmful THC (tetrahydrocannabinol) levels in the drug. THC is the chemical element of cannabis that induces the high, and levels worldwide have been growing to a dangerous extent in recent years. High THC content in cannabis variants such as skunk has been associated with a rise in drug-induced psychosis, not least among young people who are significant users of the drug. Time will tell how successful the Canadian experiment is, but in truth, it amounts to legalisation only in small part, stopping far short of the wholesale change advocated by some.

Those who oppose the idea of legalisation do so on both ideological and practical grounds. Their moral argument is not dissimilar to the one advanced as part of the War on Drugs rhetoric of the 1970s and 1980s. If we know that drugs are harmful, what message are we sending to society if we are seen to sanction their consumption? And would we not simply be encouraging a far greater number of new users – those for whom the current legal prohibitions are disincentive enough to discourage them from even trying drugs? Opponents also suggest that legalisation would not be sufficient to eliminate criminal involvement in the market. They point to the fact that there is still a significant criminal trade in cigarettes and alcohol – both of which are legal goods – not least in the form of smuggling as a means of avoiding import duties and manufacturing counterfeit versions of established brands.

But there is one thing that those on both sides of the debate agree on: current approaches simply aren't working. It is estimated that as many as one in twelve UK adults uses drugs, and there have been significant rises in children between the ages of eleven and fifteen accessing drugs. Between 2012 and 2016, there was a 77 per cent increase in the number of ten- to seventeen-year-olds convicted of possessing drugs with intent to supply them. There are still 250,000 heroin users in this country, and the growing use of synthetic drugs and so-called legal highs is simply the next in a seemingly endless list of harms.

How do you even begin to measure the full extent of that harm? Drugs destroy lives: of both addicts and casual users; of families and local neighbourhoods; of those caught up in the illicit trade – victims of trafficking and fear-filled threats and violence of the most extreme kinds. Drugs generate crime of almost every sort, enriching the wicked and ruining innocents. The economic costs of drug misuse – to the health service, to the criminal justice system, to local communities, to each and every one of us – are astonishing. The NPCC estimate that illicit drugs cost the national economy somewhere in the region of £10.7 billion every single year. That number can be broken down: the cost of drug-related acquisitive crime is estimated to be £5.8 billion; the cost of drug-related deaths and hospital admissions is estimated at £3 billion; the cost of enforcement activity is in the region of £1.1 billion. By comparison, just £0.7 billion of the total is being spent on drug treatment.[10]

But ultimately, those are just numbers. It's people who have to matter more. And the actual human cost of drugs misuse is beyond both calculation and true comprehension. I believe that it is time for a Royal Commission on drugs in this country – an old-fashioned, grown-up, robust, uncomfortable and deeply honest public conversation about the mess we're in and what to do about it. The debate needs to be driven by evidence rather than ideology, and by a sincere investigation into what actually works.

At the moment, we don't seem to be brave enough even to ask the question.

IV. *Just a Domestic*

Drugs and alcohol are undoubted drivers of devastation – in the lives of users and addicts, in their families and in the wider community. But there is, in my experience, an even greater source of damage than either of those two things, and that is violence in the home.

In England and Wales, two women every week are killed by a current or former partner: the lives of daughters, mothers, sisters, neighbours ended with shattering brutality by men of unchecked rage, men who might once have claimed to love them. But that is not all. The charity Refuge estimates that three women each week take their own lives as a consequence of having suffered from domestic violence. That's two murders and three suicides every week: more than 250 lives lost every single year.[11] Statistics published by Her Majesty's Inspectorate of Constabulary (HMIC) suggest that domestic violence and abuse account for 11 per cent of all crime committed in this country, 13 per cent of all sexual offences and fully 33 per cent of all assaults that result in an injury.[12] Those are the immediate grim realities, but the fact is that the damage caused by domestic violence extends far beyond the basic headlines and its immediate victims. It is a crime with catastrophic consequences that are passed on relentlessly through successive generations of individual families and households; a crime that retains the capacity to destroy the lives of every single person it touches. I have said it many times before, but it seems more important than ever to reiterate it here: domestic violence is terrorism on an epic scale, a disease of pandemic proportions and the single greatest cause of harm in society.

When I joined the Met in the early 1990s, domestic violence was still regarded by many people as a private matter – something that happened behind closed doors, something that was best left well alone. It was out of sight and out of mind and, frankly, most of us preferred to keep it that way. In my formative years as a PC, calls to deal with domestic violence cases were generally considered to be the source of nothing but grief. In fact, the phrase 'just another griefy domestic' had become part of the common policing vernacular. Seasoned officers were experts in finding reasons not to attend DV incidents. You would hear them on the radio saying that they were in the middle of dealing with a traffic stop, asking for someone else to be sent instead. Officers who would react in the blink of an eye to a foot chase, or suspects breaking into a house, or a pub fight would slow down and switch off when the DV calls came out. And when an officer without a ready-made excuse did eventually make it to the scene, they were met invariably either by a wall of silence or

a series of blanket denials from everyone present that anything untoward had taken place. Whatever the neighbours
might have heard through the walls was nothing more than
a minor disagreement over something trivial that had long
since blown over. Nothing going on here, Officer. If someone
appeared at the front door with visible injuries, these would
swiftly be explained away as the consequence of a slip on
the stairs or an inadvertent collision with an open cupboard
door.

On many occasions, both parties would have been drinking and neither of their slurred accounts would make much
sense. In cases where there were clear differences in the
accounts provided, it was usually one person's word against
another's, and all too often, the victim – usually female –
seemed reluctant to substantiate a formal allegation. Even if
she initially indicated willingness to give a statement and you
carted her drunken husband or boyfriend away and locked
him up for the night, she had frequently changed her mind
by the following morning. By arresting him, we had removed
the immediate threat, and with a few hours of respite to
think through her options, she seemed prepared to face the
possibility of it happening all over again. No sooner was he
released from custody than they were back together. And for
the bewildered and exasperated police officers, it meant a
whole load of paperwork for no apparent result. Really, what
was the point?

The first domestic call I ever went to was in a block of
flats just off Horseferry Road in central London. A member
of the public had called the police in response to hearing a

loud disturbance involving a warring couple who lived on the first floor. Whatever had been happening, it was over by the time we got there. She didn't appear to be hurt, and he wasn't saying much. Neither of them made any allegations, and beyond the noise heard by nearby residents (who almost certainly didn't want to be identified or to supply statements), there was no evidence of an offence having been committed. So we just turned around and walked away. I had recorded a handful of details, but the result of the call, given over the radio, went something like this:

'No offences. No further cause for police action. Pocket-book entry by PC 565AB.'

And that was it. After all, it was just a domestic. As a naïve young copper in the first year of police service, I had no concept of the overwhelming horror and endless harm caused by the violence that happens in the hidden places. But times change. And, slowly, policing experience changes you.

The first murder scene I went to was a domestic. My colleague and I were the first police unit to arrive at the scene, just off Coldharbour Lane in Brixton. I was the first police officer through the front door, and I found her face down and lifeless on the landing. I can still see all of it: the stairs that doubled back on themselves, the worn 1970s carpet, the grubby walls, the two doors leading off the corridor into the kitchen and the living room. And her – her name was Marion.

I saw her body again at the mortuary the following morning. I identified her before staying to observe the post-mortem. The pathologist revealed that she had been stabbed multiple times in the throat. The suspect, I later found out, was a former boyfriend. Someone she had trusted, perhaps even loved. It was beyond my comprehension then and it remains so now.

The second murder I went to, at the top of Brixton Hill, was a domestic too – another young woman stabbed repeatedly, this time by her current partner. He was still at the scene when my team arrived. I can recall him now, sitting on the sofa, handcuffed and silent and staring. And I remember her, coated in blood and fading away. Her name was Jane. I helped carry her to the ambulance. I stood and watched as the remarkable medical team at King's opened up her chest in a desperate and ultimately futile attempt to save her life.

I've carried the memories of those two women – of those two scenes – with me for more than twenty years. And I will carry them with me for the rest of my life.

Over time, I came to understand the truth, that it could never be 'just a domestic'. It might still be a source of significant grief, but there were lives to be saved. As a front-line PC in the 1990s, I probably attended more DV-related calls than incidents of any other kind. Not all were murder scenes, thank God, but I recognise now that all were scenes of deep sadness and desperate need: places of violence that was psychological as well as physical; violence that was repeated time and again, driven by drink and drugs and resentment and rage. In those places, I found survivors who were horrified by the prospect of staying with their partners, but terrified by the idea of leaving: victims needing urgent help, but struggling to trust those best able to offer it. Some of them were genuinely uncomprehending of the fragile state of their lives – of the very real possibility that the next attack could be terminal. Being abused was normal to them.

It is a relentless kind of harm that is happening every day, in every neighbourhood and community. If you live in a city, it is happening within a hundred yards of your front door. If you live in the country, the distance may be a little greater, but the reality is the same. Domestic violence is no respecter of gender or class or sexuality or geography. It can happen to anyone, though the fact remains that the majority of victims and survivors are women and the majority of perpetrators are men. And it is the violence against women, perpetrated by men, that I want to concentrate on here. It is not a private matter and it is not best left well alone.

My experience of attending DV murder scenes affected me deeply, far more so than I realised at the time, but attitudes and professional practice – my own and those in the wider Met – remained slow to change. In 1999, I was promoted to the rank of detective inspector and took up a post with the recently formed Racial and Violent Crime Task Force (RAVCTF), based at New Scotland Yard. The task force had been set up in the immediate aftermath of the Stephen Lawrence Inquiry, and its brief was to revolutionise the ways in which the Met dealt with race and hate crime. I will return to its anti-racism work later on, but under the broader heading of 'hate crime', the RAVCTF picked up responsibility for the police response to domestic violence.

The Met already had a service-wide domestic violence

working group that had been running for some time, but the commander who chaired it had retired and it had subsequently fallen into a certain amount of disrepair. As I started my new job, it was clear that nobody really wanted to take the group on. At the Yard, I bore witness to the HQ equivalent of the response-team PCs who used to do all they could to avoid the DV-related radio calls. A succession of officers more senior than me indicated that they had other priorities to deal with and couldn't possibly take anything else on. Eventually it fell to me, as the new boy, to accept responsibility.

To be honest, I was as reluctant as the rest of them. Though the experience of dealing with DV murders had undoubtedly left its mark, domestic violence itself was still not a subject I felt especially strongly about. I was certain that there was more interesting and important work to be done, and the lack of a queue to take ownership of the working group seemed to offer a reasonable indication of the level of importance the organisation was attaching to the issue. I was four ranks junior to the commander who had been in charge before me, and I had nothing to draw upon apart from my operational experience of responding to DV. I had never been involved in any kind of policy work before and I had never sat on a corporate board, much less chaired one. But it turned out to be a life-changing experience – both a privilege and an education.

The working group had around a dozen loyal members, most of them drawn from outside policing. One or two of them had their own lived experience of domestic violence, and several of them had many years of professional experience supporting survivors, working for remarkable charities such as Refuge and Women's Aid. These were people who really knew and understood what they were talking about, who were passionate about seeing change, and who taught me lessons that I have never forgotten. Quite apart from anything else, they taught me the facts – the stark realities – of this most hideous of crimes.

With the help of the working group, I began to understand some of the complex reasons why victims might be reluctant to report incidents and crimes to the police. It all begins with fear – a kind of fear that is many layered and overwhelming. First is the (well-founded and perfectly understandable) fear of their abuser. They are afraid of the next brutal attack and they are afraid that any attempt to contact the police will be met with terrible retribution. To put it bluntly, they are afraid that their partner is going to kill them. But that's just the beginning. They are also afraid of losing their children, their rationale being that if they tell the police, then the police will tell Social Services and Social Services are going to come and take their kids away.

Whether or not those concerns are well founded, many women would rather risk further abuse than risk losing their families. But what kind of choice is that? And it's not just their children they are frightened of losing, it's also their homes and their financial security. It's the easiest thing in the world to say to a DV survivor, 'Why don't you just leave him?' But it's never that simple. To start with, where would she go? And how would she provide for her family? In any case, what is there to stop her former partner tracking her down and taking his revenge? These women are not weak or somehow clueless. In fact, they are some of the smartest, bravest human beings you could ever meet, finding ways to survive in circumstances that you and I can scarcely believe, much less understand, caught endlessly between the fear of dying and the fear of losing everything.

The situation is made worse still by the realisation that many of them don't trust those in positions of authority. The police and Social Services, in particular, are viewed frequently with a level of suspicion that borders on hostility.

The further disturbing reality is that some women actually believe that the abuse is their fault – that, for reasons I can't begin to fathom, they somehow had it coming to them. It happened because she burned his dinner, or was late home from work, or wore an outfit he didn't like, or because his football team had lost. Almost anything might set him off. These are the women who somehow find a way to blame themselves for the violence of men. And some of them can be attacked on dozens of occasions before the police are called for the first time. DV has by far the highest rate of repeat victimisation of any crime committed in this country.

*

Not long ago, I caught up with a friend who is still a serving detective in the Met. Based in south London, she has extensive experience as a DV investigator. As we chatted over a bite to eat, she told me the story of a young woman in her early twenties called Eleanor.

My friend and her police colleagues first met Eleanor after

she had started a relationship with a man who was much older than her. Though she might not have known it when she first met him, he was exceptionally dangerous, with a long history of serious domestic violence offending. His ex-wife and her four children had managed to escape and had started to rebuild their lives, but most of his crimes had gone unreported. The police – and Eleanor – only found out about them much later on.

Eleanor was next in line. Initially, there had been just the suggestion of a couple of apparently minor assaults, and one or two calls from concerned local residents, but he was never charged. Then one day he attacked her outside the flat where they lived, prompting a neighbour to try to intervene. So he assaulted the neighbour as well. Not being trapped in the abusive relationship, the neighbour had no hesitation in calling the police and giving a statement. The man was convicted at court, but Eleanor chose to remain with him.

By this time, the local police DV intervention team had been made aware of her circumstances and had tried to offer support. They recognised the level of risk she was facing and issued her with a panic button that she was able to carry hidden in her bra. Even as I type that last sentence, I find it astonishing that in a city like London in the early part of the twenty-first century, some women still live in such fear that they have to conceal an alarm in their underwear. What does that say about who we are?

A couple of weeks later, her partner assaulted her again, strangling her in an attack so ferocious she thought she was going to die. Somehow, she managed to get away from him, but made the decision once again not to report the crime to the police. Instead, she simply stayed clear of him overnight, before going to meet some friends for a drink the following day.

Inevitably, he found out where she was and went after her. Eleanor and her friends were sitting in a group at the back of a pub and she didn't see him when he first came in. He bought a drink, then, without saying a word, sat down near the bar and stared at her. Put like that, it might not sound like much of anything, but my friend had viewed the pub CCTV and described to me just how chillingly sinister his behaviour was. He knew exactly what he was doing. It was all about fear and intimidation and coercive control. He sat and he stared until, eventually, she realised he was there.

In front of all her friends, he started to turn on the charm. They thought he was wonderful, and, feeling as though she had no choice, she left the pub with him. But as soon as they got outside, she knew she was in real danger. She ducked into a nearby newsagent and tried to ask the shopkeeper to call for help. Her abuser followed her in, so she pressed her panic alarm and ran out into the street. He grabbed hold of her and threw her against the shop window.

The police got there in time, the man was arrested and Eleanor provided an initial statement. But then she refused to sign it. It was apparent that she was absolutely terrified of him. My friend worked twenty hours straight to try to put together a case and ensure he was kept in custody. She understood the simple fact that her efforts during those hours might mean the difference between life and death for

Eleanor. She had no victim statement that she could use, the CCTV from the shop was poor quality and the shopkeeper wasn't much help. But she had the panic alarm activation and the text of a 999 call from a witness, and she had the man's previous history of offending. Through sheer determination, she managed to assemble enough evidence to charge him with ABH and have him remanded. He was later sentenced to six months in prison – no small achievement given the inherent complexities involved in any case of intimate partner violence.

During the period he was in prison, my friend and her colleagues kept in close touch with Eleanor, and the more Eleanor trusted, the more she confided. She told my friend about the hospital visits and the broken bones, and she gave permission for the police to access her medical records. They told a tale of horrifying abuse. But when the moment came, she was still unable to sign an evidential statement. My friend described sitting alongside her as she held the pen with shaking hands. She just couldn't do it.

When Eleanor's abuser was released from prison, he found her – despite the fact that she was living in a new flat – and moved back in with her. 'He might have changed,' she said. But then fate intervened. While my friend was still trying to work out what to do to protect Eleanor, the man's former wife came forward and substantiated a series of exceptionally serious allegations against him. She had been given time and space to mend – and to understand what kind of man he really was. She provided clear evidence of repeated physical violence and sexual assault. He had beaten her and he had raped her and he had shown no remorse. The judge sentenced him to eighteen years in jail.

I asked my friend what the greatest reward had been in all her time working as a DV investigator. Her answer was immediate and straightforward: 'I know for a fact that I saved some people's lives.' And I don't doubt that Eleanor was one of them. But before we parted, I also asked her about the burdens she bore as a DV investigator. She mentioned two particular things. First was the overwhelming volume of work – an extraordinary number of active investigations and pending court cases, as well as the new prisoners who appear in the cells every day of the week, always knowing that each DV assault victim has the potential to be the next murder victim. The second burden was the sad realisation – in her words, 'soul-destroying' – that there are some people you might not be able to save.

Eleanor had written to the police to thank them for saving her life. But not long into his eighteen-year sentence, she began visiting her abuser in prison. And she told my friend that once he was released, they were going to get back together again. People are endlessly complex. But while the choices and decisions some of us make can seem incomprehensible to others, we must never lose sight of the truth that no victim is ever to blame for the violence committed against them. That responsibility rests with the perpetrator alone.

*

A year or so after starting out with the DV working group, it was time for me to move on. I put my uniform back on and was asked to take charge of an emergency response team in west London. Returning to the front line, I realised that my understanding of – and consequently my attitude towards – domestic violence had changed completely. When I noticed that some local officers were still slower to respond to DV calls than they were to many other emergencies, I tried to pass on the things I'd learned. I tried to explain to them why domestic violence matters so much.

I told them about the two women who are murdered every week, and emphasised the fact that an effective response to DV is an essential means of homicide prevention. I reminded them that before anything else, their job was to save lives. I also told them that an effective response to DV was a means of reducing many forms of serious crime – violent crime in particular. But as well as making a hard-nosed, crime-related business case, I talked to them about the basic humanitarian reasons for doing what needed to be done. Getting our response to domestic violence right was about defending and protecting some of the most vulnerable people in our communities, while at the same time confronting and challenging some of the most violent and dangerous criminals in society.

While I went back to working on a response team, my former colleagues at the Racial and Violent Crime Task Force had overseen the establishment of community safety units (CSUs) in every London borough – thirty-two dedicated race and hate crime investigation teams, ring-fenced from any other form of investigatory work. Many stations had previously employed specialist domestic violence investigators – brilliant officers, wholly committed to their cause – but the introduction of CSUs represented a new level of training and investment. The Met was putting its money where its mouth was.

Over time, local boroughs also began working much more closely with partner agencies, both in local government and in the charitable sector, recognising that the police alone were never going to succeed in addressing the demands of DV. With a growing understanding of the reasons why so many victims were reluctant to talk to the police, officers worked alongside independent domestic violence advisers (IDVAs) who were able to provide direct support to victims and survivors, building a rapport and remaining with them through any criminal justice process that might follow.

When I later took over as borough commander for Camden in 2010, the IDVAs were located alongside the CSU, on the ground floor at Holborn police station. It was Camden CSU officers who undertook one of the earliest victimless prosecutions – charging a DV offender and taking him to court even though his seriously injured victim had been unwilling to provide a statement.

Over the course of the first decade of the twenty-first century, the police response to domestic violence changed beyond recognition. But for all the progress made, the harsh fact remains that the challenge is as great as it ever was. Eleanor's story is evidence of that fact. The truth is that one in four women in this country will experience domestic violence at some point in her lifetime. In the year ending March 2017, 1.2 million women in England and Wales reported experiencing domestic violence and abuse of one form or another.[13] Pause and think about that number, just for a moment. It is staggering. But what makes it even worse is the fact that it is undoubtedly a significant underestimate. Domestic violence remains a largely hidden crime, and huge numbers of victims and survivors are either unable or unwilling to speak out about what is happening to them. HMIC quote figures estimating that less than 24 per cent of DV-related crime is reported to the police. And yet the police still receive a DV-related call every thirty seconds – two a minute, 120 every single hour. And any one of those could be to a murder.[14]

According to Refuge, domestic violence costs the UK economy somewhere in the region of £23 billion every year.[15] But I rarely find myself thinking about the money. I think instead about Marion and Jane, and all the others like them. I wonder whether we might have been able to do something to save them, if not on the day of their murders, then in the days and weeks beforehand. I wonder at the extent of the violence and abuse they endured – the punches, the kicks, the verbal abuse and taunts, the slaps, the sexual assaults – before the knives were drawn. One estimate provided by Refuge suggests that 73 per cent of all DV incidents are experienced by repeat victims.[16]

Between 2014 and 2016, HMIC conducted a series of DV-related reviews of every police force in England and Wales. They noted a number of improvements in the police response to domestic violence, not least in the assessment of risk faced by survivors and in the positive action taken with regard to alleged perpetrators (for example, making an arrest irrespective of whether or not a signed statement had been provided). They also noted that there had been a 61 per cent increase in the reporting of domestic violence and abuse, much of which was attributed to improvements in the police approach to dealing with and recording DV crimes, and to victims having greater confidence to report those crimes in the knowledge that their allegations would be taken seriously.[17] That can only be a good thing, but it also represented a huge increase in demand on police time and capacity, just at the point where the impact of government funding cuts to policing was biting deepest. It meant fewer officers with fewer resources trying to cope with higher caseloads and greater levels of risk than ever before.

It's not just in policing that these economic realities have been felt so deeply. Writing in the *Guardian* in October 2018, Isabel Hardman pointed out that since 2011, local government cuts had resulted in a 31 per cent reduction in cash support for front-line support services run by one national DV charity, something that had had a direct and immediate impact on DV survivors. For example, the inevitable gaps in funding had led to such a shortage of secure accommodation that as many as ninety women (and a similar number of children) were being turned away from refuges – from possible places of safety – on any one day.[18] The violence of austerity compounding the violence of life.

Though we might have come a long way as a society in understanding the impact that DV has on its immediate victims and survivors, we have barely begun to consider its secondary impact on the children who are being born into and growing up in the homes where the violence is happening.

Research quoted by the *Daily Telegraph* in early 2019 estimates that one in five children in the UK has been exposed to domestic violence.[19] These children are witnesses to it and they are victims of it. The National Society for the Prevention of Cruelty to Children (NSPCC) estimate that up to 250,000 children are living in violent homes.[20] The early-years exposure to violence – and to the extreme trauma that is an inevitable consequence of it – has repercussions that last a lifetime. The story of the writer Erwin James is evidence of that.

In the spring of 2018, I was invited to speak at a literary festival being hosted in the beautiful grounds of Chiddingstone Castle in Kent. I was due to be interviewed alongside Erwin, who had recently published an immensely powerful memoir, *Redeemable*.

Erwin was born in 1957 to extremely poor itinerant Scottish parents, and his early years were marked by tragedy and trauma. When he was just seven years old, his mother, Jeannie, died in a car crash after its drunk driver lost control of the vehicle and collided with a lamp post. Erwin's father was sitting in the back and was hospitalised with serious injuries. And in that moment of roadside impact, Erwin's life changed for ever.

He describes being disturbed from his sleep late that night by a knock on the front door. He looked out of the window to see a police car parked out front and officers standing on the doorstep. He listened to the hushed conversation and he heard his grandmother's screams. But no one came to talk to him, and so he curled up under the bedcovers and cried himself to sleep.

He goes on to describe his father's subsequent return from hospital and the heavy drinking that began almost straight away. 'My father came and went on his crutches, sometimes not returning for days at a time. When he was home, he drank more and punched holes in the doors, shouting "Jeannie! Jeannie!" Once he punched the wall so hard, he broke his hand and had to go back to hospital. He was drunk more often than he was sober.'

To begin with, young Erwin somehow found a way to deal with his father's drinking and consequent behaviour, but everything changed when his dad turned on his new partner, Stella. 'He punched her and he kicked her. We heard him roaring at her ... Stella screamed in pain, in fear. One night the fighting sounded like it was going up the stairs. Bodies were hitting against the walls.'

Eventually, his father was sent to prison. While he was behind bars, Erwin became involved in petty crime. When his dad was released and later caught him stealing, he attacked his son, punching and kicking him repeatedly. On another occasion, he threatened to kill Erwin. Unsurprisingly, the young boy's life unravelled. Writing in the *Guardian* in April 2009, Erwin reflected on his childhood. 'I had lived an itinerant, dysfunctional existence from a very young age. For a number of years, I had been subjected to serious violence and emotional deprivation ... By the age of ten, I was running wild, sleeping rough.'

Erwin was separated from his beloved younger sister when she was tiny. He stumbled from one broken-home setting to the next, in and out of education and, repeatedly, into low-level criminality. Then his father found a new partner, Carlene, and the beatings began all over again.

Just before his eleventh birthday, Erwin was arrested for breaking into a sweetshop. Convicted of burglary, he was put into care. He ran away on numerous occasions, sleeping rough while continuing to commit crime. Over time, this broken young man began to repeat the patterns of his childhood.

'For me, it was no big deal to get drunk, have a fight, smash a window or steal a car. It was just a way of life. I never thought of the people I was inconveniencing, never considered the impact my antisocial behaviour was having on others. I had two spells in youth prisons six months in a detention centre and a year in Borstal. Each time I was released I was full of good intentions, but each time I sank rapidly back into my earlier destructive and directionless way of life.

'As my frustration with a life without purpose increased, my recklessness and lack of concern for others intensified. Drunkenness and violence became established character traits. By the time I was in my early twenties I had left behind two serious relationships that had broken down due to my alcohol-fuelled, violent behaviour, and I was well and truly adrift.'

In 1984, Erwin murdered two men. And in 1985, the judge in Number 1 Court at the Old Bailey sentenced him to life for his crimes. He remained in prison for two decades, written off by the world.

I liked Erwin from the moment I met him. He was thick-set, gentle and softly spoken. In a quiet room tucked away from the festival crowds, he took my hand, looked me in the eye and told me that he was glad to meet me. I told him that the pleasure was mine, and introduced him to my wife, Bear, and our three children. With time and space to talk, we discovered that we had a great deal in common – a love of *The Lion, the Witch and the Wardrobe*, a passion for writing, a desire to make a positive difference in the world. When our time came, we walked out to the marquee and took our places to tell our stories.

He talked openly about his 'very painful life', about becoming a 'dysfunctional character' and about the selfish, predatory nature of his behaviour. He talked about hating the fact that he was a criminal, and the three questions he asked of himself: Was I born bad? Did I become bad? Did I choose to be bad? He wanted to understand how he became what he became.

He explained that his life had been transformed by meeting a prison psychologist called Joan Branton. She worked on a wing that housed eighty-five murderers, including serial killers, but she chose not to define them by their crimes. She didn't see Erwin as he saw himself, and she began to teach him that, contrary to every instinct and belief he held, he was redeemable. She explained to him that 'understanding is not the same as excusing', and with her gentle help, he began to unravel the carnage and chaos of his life.

Erwin has never made the slightest attempt to excuse what he did. In fact, he is lacerating in his description of his own sense of guilt and it is clear that he will carry that burden with him for the rest of his life. 'There are people still grieving because of me ... there are two people who are not here because of me,' he told the audience in the castle grounds. In his *Guardian* piece, he wrote: 'If the death penalty had been on the statute books I would have deserved to be executed. But I had been sentenced to life, so I had to live.'

With Joan's steady help, he began to understand that, while he alone was responsible for his criminal acts, he was certainly not responsible for the catastrophes of his childhood. She taught him that he had been born lovable, with the potential to become all that he was meant to be. The truth was that he was not to blame for the brokenness, violence and trauma that had dominated his early years. It wasn't his fault.

Understanding is not the same as excusing, but it is the beginning of healing. Here was a man with a past marked by horror and shame but a present and future marked by redemption and hope. Erwin James is my friend. I'm immensely proud to call him that. But I mourn the fact that his story – of the long-term consequences of childhood exposure to extreme violence and trauma – is far from unique. Unchecked, the harm caused by domestic violence has the potential to go on forever.

*

If any prime minister or Home Secretary were ever to ask me – on the basis of all my years as a police officer – which type of crime we should prioritise ahead of any other, I would say without hesitation domestic violence.

Britain needs a long-term domestic violence plan, one that recognises both the urgency and the complexity of the situation; one that addresses fully the shattering harm done both to immediate victims and survivors and to the children who are growing up in the places where it's happening. I believe that any suspect who assaults their partner in the presence or hearing of her children should automatically be guilty of an assault on those children too. We need a plan that is safeguarded from the vagaries of changing political priorities and from the worst that austerity can do; one that also insists on the provision of effective perpetrator programmes, compelling men to confront the reality and consequences of their violent behaviour and providing them with support to change the way the live their lives. More than anything, though, we need a plan that recognises the fact that there is nothing that matters more than saving lives.

When I was growing up, people smoked in pubs and restaurants, none of us wore seat belts, most of us didn't give a second thought to the idea of climate change, and men battered women behind closed doors. These days, my children think that anyone who smokes is an idiot, the first thing we do when we get in the car is put our seat belts on, and the global warming sceptics are the ones in denial. There is only one thing on that childhood list that is still to change.

It is long past time.

V. *On a Knife Edge*

In early 2007, a succession of teenagers were murdered in a series of unconnected attacks across London – six in the first two months of the year alone. Three of them were shot, three of them were stabbed. Two of the victims were just fifteen years old, and the oldest was only eighteen.

Children were dying.

Alongside the mainstream media coverage, MTV broadcast a *News Special* highlighting the growing public concern about the violence, and about knife crime in particular. The programme featured an interview with a boy called Kodjo Yenga – a sixteen-year-old A-level student from a loving home, a refugee from the Congo who had never been in contact, much less trouble, with the police. But he had his fears, and they were captured by the camera: 'I think stabbings are getting worse. I don't think it happens all the time but it happens quite a lot.'

At about 5 p.m. on Wednesday 14 March 2007, it happened to him. Kodjo was attacked and killed by a group of youths in Hammersmith Grove, west London. There was no obvious reason for the crime. The confrontation in the street – in which he was undoubtedly a reluctant participant – might have had something to do with the fleeting and indistinct notion of 'respect', but that was about all the police were ever able to identify as a motive for his murder. Kodjo died from a single stab wound to his heart. At the time, I was in charge of community policing in the neighbourhood where it happened, and my mobile phone rang with the news. Another one dead. In the painful weeks that followed, a boy I had never met became a boy I will never forget.

The following day, I visited the scene. I saw the sea of flowers, messages, candles and photographs crowding the pavements and walls on an affluent street corner where things like this just didn't happen. Standing next to the senior investigating officer from the murder team, I faced the line-up of live television cameras and the inquisition of the journalists stationed beside them: 'Is this now a full-blown epidemic?' 'Have the police lost control of the streets?' 'Surely we need more stop and search?' 'Is it not time to be calling for longer jail terms for those caught carrying knives?'

Closed questions, characteristic of those I would be asked repeatedly by reporters over the course of the next decade. Closed minds. Almost nobody asked about the reasons why it was actually happening. In any case, within a day or two, the attention of the media would almost certainly be elsewhere. At least until the next boy fell.

The following weekend, I was back in Hammersmith Grove, watching from a respectful distance as Kodjo's mother, accompanied by family and friends and members of her church congregation, visited the scene. I listened to them sing. I listened to them wail. And my heart broke for them. By the end of 2007, twenty-seven teenagers had been murdered in the capital in one year – eighteen of them stabbed, eight of them shot and one of them beaten to death. And there is a danger that we forget their names; that they just become numbers, another bleak pin on the murder map of London. But that will never be the case for those who were there, or for the families who grieve. The journalist Andrew Anthony, writing in a feature for the *Observer*, recorded the simple, plaintive words of Ladjua Lesele, Kodjo's mother: 'I have no life any more.'

Who can begin to comprehend the depth of a parent's grief? And how were we going to respond to the senseless loss of another innocent life? These were the questions that troubled me both professionally and personally.

As I began to absorb the full sadness of Kodjo's death, I knew that it wasn't enough to respond as we had always done in the past, with monotone calls for more enforcement and tougher sentencing. Those things have their part to play, of course, but they aren't the long-term solution to anything. I knew that we had a responsibility to go far deeper – to try to understand why the hell a young man would pick up a knife in the first place, much less be inclined to use it. I sat down with colleagues from the local authority and we took the collective decision to examine in exhaustive detail the backgrounds of a group of thirteen young people who were suspected of being present at the scene of Kodjo's murder. We searched every available database and every other possible source of information, looking to identify whether there were any common factors in their life stories, anything that might serve as a possible indicator or predictor of the propensity for deadly violence. We knew that we had a responsibility to try to understand why some children become killers, and these were the facts we found:

Eleven of the group of suspects were boys, two were girls. All of them were teenagers, some as young as thirteen.

Twelve of them came from single-parent homes: Mum was there, but Dad was nowhere. The thirteenth child was living with a parent and a step-parent – referred to clumsily in one of the official documents as a 'reconstituted family'.

Eight of them were attending secondary school, three were on the books at the local pupil referral unit (a facility for those who were excluded from mainstream education) and two weren't in any kind of school at all. At least eight had a previous record of school exclusions (in three of the remaining five cases, there was no information available).

Eleven of the thirteen had a record of previous involvement with Social Services and ten of them had a history of offending and contact with the local Youth Offending Service. At least four of them had older brothers with serious criminal records.

Most of them came from economically poor households: seven of the thirteen were eligible for free school meals. Poor children from poor households who were disadvantaged from the very start.

But as we reviewed the findings, there was one fact that stood out to me above all the others. We were told that every one of the suspect group had been raised in a violent home. They had been either victims of or witnesses to domestic violence and abuse. And there didn't appear to be a single exception. That simple fact remains one of the most significant and unsettling discoveries of my policing career. The desperate truth seems to be that those who are exposed to violence in childhood are at greater risk of expressing violence in adolescence and young adulthood. Remember my friend Erwin James.

Back in 2007, I didn't have the right language for it, but these days people speak of the reality and consequences of what are now known as ACEs – adverse childhood experiences. Public Health England describe the three direct and six indirect factors that have a significant impact on a child's early-years development.[11] The direct factors are grouped under the heading 'Child Maltreatment' and are as follows:

- verbal abuse
- physical abuse
- sexual abuse

Three phrases that trip off the page easily enough, representing a whole world of pain.

The indirect factors set out by Public Health England are those present in the household where the child is growing up:

- parental separation
- domestic violence
- mental illness

- alcohol abuse
- drug use
- parental imprisonment

At the heart of everything is trauma. The greater a child's exposure to trauma, the greater the risks to their physical, emotional and mental health – and the greater the likely adverse consequences for their overall life chances. Public Health England quote research suggesting that, when compared with people who have suffered no ACEs, those who have been exposed to four or more are:

- two times more likely to have a poor diet
- three times more likely to smoke
- five times more likely to have had sex under 16 years
- two times more likely to binge drink
- seven times more likely to have been involved in recent violence
- eleven times more likely to have been incarcerated
- eleven times more likely to have used heroin or crack cocaine

In addition, 64 per cent of those in contact with substance misuse services and 50 per cent of homeless people have had four or more ACEs.

Exposure to trauma even has profound implications for a child's brain development, including significant adverse consequences for the development of nervous, hormonal and immunological systems.

The lists of ACEs and their consequences make for devastating reading. And the stories of the children who were present when Kodjo was killed can be read all the way through them. Five of the boys in the group were eventually convicted of his murder. Two of them were thirteen years old on the day it happened; the oldest was just sixteen. All of them had been exposed to violence in their childhoods. All of them came from broken homes. All of them came from economically poor backgrounds. All of them had been excluded from school in the past for using or threatening violence, towards either a fellow pupil or a member of staff. Four of the five had previous criminal convictions, with at least one of them being on court bail at the time Kodjo was killed. The records of some of them show concerns regarding both mental health and drug use. Deprived kids, from violent, broken homes, replaying the patterns of their own lives in the death of another. It's almost as though we could have predicted what was going to happen in Hammersmith on that March afternoon.

*

In the early hours of Sunday 29 June 2008, Ben Kinsella was stabbed to death on the streets of Islington, north London. He was sixteen years old and had been out for the evening with friends, celebrating the end of GCSE exams. Like Kodjo, Ben had never been in trouble with the police. He was described by his family as 'a normal teenager who loved art, music, football and girls'. Three boys, two of them aged eighteen and one aged nineteen at the time of the attack, were convicted of his murder.

On the afternoon of Wednesday 20 April 2011, twenty-two-year-old Milad Golmakani was stabbed to death in Camden, north London. His seventeen-year-old friend survived the attack. Milad suffered fourteen stab wounds to his neck, chest and back. At the murder trial, the Home Office pathologist described the ferocious blows that had cut through bone, severed arteries and pierced his lungs. The post-mortem examination had discovered two litres of blood in his left chest cavity. Four teenagers were sentenced to life in prison for his murder.

On Sunday 30 December 2012, seventeen-year-old Dogan Ismail was stabbed to death on the Aylesbury Estate in Southwark, south London. He had been trying to retrieve a mobile phone that had been stolen from his younger brother a couple of days before. A fifteen-year-old boy was convicted of his murder. At his trial, the judge made particular reference to the 'force and ferocity' of the attack.

Ben and Milad and Dogan – two children and one young man. There were many others during that time, of course, but these three were killed in parts of London where I happened to be working at the time – in places where I was supposed to be in charge.

In the days following each murder, journalists tended to ask the same things as before. The first question put to me by the BBC reporter as we walked through the Aylesbury Estate, the scene of Dogan's murder, was about whether the police had lost control in the local area. Most politicians did much the same. For more than ten years, I found myself having almost identical conversations with the people in positions of power and influence – the people best placed to identify and act upon the urgent need for change. I tried to move the debate along – from limited conversations about greater enforcement to much more informed debates about the underlying reasons for what was happening – but rarely with much success. When the cameras stopped rolling at the scene, I would take the journalist to one side and offer to assist with a longer feature, anything that might begin to look at the real causes and possible solutions to it all. The initial response would be positive, but then I would hear nothing back from them. They had their headline and their sound bite, and it was on to the next thing.

Looking at London as a whole, it is tempting to conclude that nothing really changed in all those years – apart, that is, from the names of the dead. Attention from those on the outside came and went. Interest from those not directly affected ebbed and flowed. But in the real lives of real people in poor neighbourhoods and troubled homes, nothing changed at all. It might even be argued that, in the context of the overwhelming damage done by austerity, things actually got worse.

Meanwhile, north of the border, the story was a very different one. In the early 2000s, Scotland had an unenviable reputation. In 2005, a United Nations report identified it as the country with the greatest number of violent assaults in the developed world. In the same year, the World Health Organisation published figures suggesting that Glasgow was 'the murder capital of Europe'. While the context and some of the detail was very different to London, the challenge was essentially the same: how to stem the flow of blood.

Strathclyde Police (now part of Police Scotland) understood that a very different approach was required. And so, in early 2005, they set up the Glasgow Violence Reduction Unit (VRU). The VRU website describes their founding aim: 'to target all forms of violent behaviour, in particular knife crime and weapon carrying among young men in and around Glasgow'. And their methodology represented a radical departure from anything that had gone before. They adopted the view that violence was at least as much a health issue as it was a crime issue. Violence, they said, was a disease – one that could be caught and transmitted. To quote from a *Guardian* article published in July 2018: 'Beyond the obvious health problems resulting from violence – the physical injuries and psychological trauma – the violent behaviour itself is an epidemic that spreads from person to person.'[22]

But diseases can also be diagnosed. They can be treated, and they might even be prevented. So Strathclyde became the first police force in the world to adopt a public health approach to violence. Two of the founders and central figures in the development of the work of the VRU were Karyn McCluskey and John Carnochan – she a senior police analyst, he a senior police officer. They began by trying to understand the drivers of violence in Scotland, identifying a series of powerful factors – poverty, inequality and alcohol abuse, for example – that were far beyond the influence, never mind control, of policing. As a consequence, they recognised the need to develop as broad an alliance of partners as possible.

Knife crime wasn't just about policing. It was a whole-society problem that demanded whole-society solutions.

They worked with partners in health and education and they worked with local Jobcentres – 'nothing stops a bullet like a job', they said, echoing a view expressed by violence reduction experts in America. They trained GPs, dentists and even vets to identify the signs of violence and to offer life-saving support to those at greatest risk of harm. In 2008, three Glasgow surgeons set up the independent charity Medics Against Violence (MAV), with the aim of helping to prevent young people from being killed or seriously injured. Dr Christine Goodall, a consultant oral surgeon and one of the three MAV founders, explained her motivation for getting involved: 'I had seen significant numbers of young people injured as a result of violence... I realised we were very good at treating their injuries but we were not so good at dealing with the root causes. We were doing nothing to prevent these injuries, that had to change... People sometimes ask me, "So why is a dentist doing all this?" My reply is, "Why not?" Somebody had to do it. We all had a role to play.'[23] MAV's education and training work includes an award-winning secondary schools programme that allows health professionals to engage directly with pupils in addressing both the causes and the consequences of violence.

The VRU worked with a coalition of the willing – anyone who might possibly be able to make a difference. And they were successful. More than a decade after the formation of the unit, recorded crime in Scotland was at a forty-year low. The murder rate in Glasgow had fallen by 60 per cent.

Between 2006 and 2011, there were fifteen teenage knife murders in Glasgow. From 2011 to 2016, there were none. Violence remains a significant challenge in Scotland, domestic violence in particular, but lives have undoubtedly been saved, and the country is no longer host to the murder capital of Europe.

There are three immediate and powerful lessons that I take from the experience of the VRU. The first is the simple truth that violence does not have to be inevitable. The second is that the achievement of any meaningful change requires extraordinary levels of patience – of the kind that is so often in short supply in this frantic, flat-out world of ours. The third lesson is that violence reduction can never be just about policing; that policing is just one part of a much larger, much more complicated puzzle. Violence is preventable, but it will take time and it will take all of us.

South of the border, we still have some catching up to do. In 2018, the Conservative Home Secretary announced the launch of a public health approach to dealing with violence in England and Wales. At about the same time, the Labour Mayor of London announced the creation of a violence reduction unit in London. The City Hall VRU began its work in the capital in 2019, and at the same time, a number of other regional VRUs were established. Only time will tell whether these tentative steps actually amount to anything. I don't doubt the commitment of the police officers and other professionals involved, but in my repeated experience, politicians have a habit of making policy statements about things that appear to matter to voters at a particular moment in time, before rapidly losing interest as soon as a more pressing political fire starts in their backyards. In London, the knee-jerk response to the latest stabbing is still so often to resort to the same closed questions as before – blaming the police for the problem while simultaneously making them almost entirely responsible for fixing it. And I promise you that approach is never going to succeed.

We need to adopt the same kind of far-sighted approach to knife crime as we do to domestic violence. I would go so far as to suggest that London needs a twenty-year knife crime plan – one that recognises the breadth, depth and complexity of the challenge we're facing. And as with any effective plan, it needs short-, medium- and long-term components.

The short-term is all about murder suppression. As borough commander in Southwark, my briefing to officers in the days and weeks following Dogan Ismail's murder was as simple as it could be: 'I want you out there saving lives.'

That really was the only message, and it required extensive levels of proactive enforcement activity. With the engagement and support of the local community, we significantly increased the local use of police stop and search powers – just at the time when most other parts of London (indeed, most other parts of the country) were significantly reducing theirs. Stop and search remains the subject of a wearying binary debate between those who appear to regard it as the answer to every ill in society and those who view it as the root of all evil. Both perspectives are wrong, but it seems almost impossible to have any kind of intelligent, nuanced public conversation about the subject. Wagons get circled, protagonists retreat behind tired language and stereotypical points of view and no one seems willing to give any ground.

My professional experience is unequivocal: in the short-term, stop and search saves lives. I have seen it first-hand, time and time again, in different neighbourhoods in north, south and west London. In those places, I have spent time with local people – old and young alike – who understand the need for the police to use their stop and search powers. Their only concern has been about the way in which the powers are used. They want the police to search people but, crucially, they want it done professionally, with courtesy and respect. And I am in absolute agreement with them. The first duty and greatest privilege that any police officer will ever have is to save lives, and stop and search helps them to do that. Just at this moment in time, there are some young men out on our streets who are so dangerous that there is no alternative but to confront them and lock them up. But we need to be equally clear about the fact that enforcement alone is never going to fix anything.

In the medium-term, London's twenty-year plan needs to focus on engagement and intervention, on efforts to offer people on otherwise predictable paths the opportunity to change the way they live their lives. The Scottish VRU employed 'navigators', often individuals with their own lived experience of violence and its consequences, to work directly with those at risk of becoming involved in serious violence themselves. In Chicago, a city that offered much of the inspiration for the VRU, they deploy 'violence interrupt-ers' into troubled neighbourhoods to work with known gang members and those identified as at risk of being drawn into potentially deadly local conflicts. After Ben Kinsella's murder in Islington, we set up a Youth Engagement Team – five officers with particular skills and experience in working with young people. When a stabbing happened, we deployed them as part of the emergency response – alongside youth workers from the local authority – into the area where the attack had taken place. Their job was to prevent escalation and reprisals by intervening directly with young people out on the street. On the days when there were no stabbings, they went out on proactive patrol, not to stop and search, but to stop and talk. Because communication is the beginning of resolution.

The charity Red Thread works in a number of London's A&E departments. Their youth workers are able to intervene in the cases where victims have been rushed into hospital after being stabbed. They describe the 'teachable moment' when young men realise, perhaps for the very first time, the real life – and death – consequences of the path they've chosen. In that moment, they might just be prepared to listen to the voice of someone willing and able to save them. A second charity, Divert, operates on a similar principle in a number of the Met's custody centres. A young person is arrested for carrying a knife, and while the usual criminal justice process runs its course, a youth worker will spend time with them, presenting them with a variety of education, training and employment opportunities as realistic alternatives to a life of crime.

There are those who decry these sorts of interventions as being somehow soft on crime. But that's nonsense. These are clear-headed, evidenced-based, pragmatic responses to an overwhelming problem. When the Scottish VRU first started operating, there was still a heavy emphasis on the necessity of enforcement. But the longer they continued, the less that requirement remained, because fewer boys were being stabbed and killed.

Short-term murder suppression, medium-term engagement and intervention. The long-term element of London's twenty-year plan needs to focus on transformation. That means adopting a genuine public health approach – not just as a convenient sound bite, but as a fundamentally different way of doing things. Violence is infinitely more complicated than we want it to be, and it follows that the answers to violence are too. To begin with, an effective health approach will need a proper understanding of the difference between the symptoms, the aggravators and the causes of the kinds of life stories that end with the blade of a knife.

Gang membership – in the cases where it exists and appears to be a factor – is, in my view, more often a symptom than a cause. It is a deeply troubling sign of the absence or loss of basic human connection. Gangs are so often the last stop on the journey for those from broken families (or no families at all) who are searching for somewhere to belong. Joining a gang places a young person at greater risk of violence than not belonging to one, but that kind of logic is lost in the search for a place to call home.

Problematic drug use – for example, smoking high-strength cannabis (often referred to as 'skunk'), and the increased risk of associated psychosis – is frequently more of a symptom too. It might be seen as a search for comfort in a world of no comfort at all; a desire for numbness in a world where feeling anything is just too painful. Even violence itself can be a source of comfort for some.

I have a good friend, Dr Charlie Howard, who is a clinical psychologist. For as long as I have known her, she has been working on the streets with some of the most challenged and challenging people. Years ago, she told me the story of one young man she had been spending time with. Let's call him Shaun. Sometimes Shaun found himself out on the streets actively looking for a fight. Terrifyingly, he told her that it had become the only way he knew to keep himself calm. As Charlie dug deeper, she discovered that he had grown up experiencing horrific levels of domestic violence. At first, he had found it frightening, but over time, he had come to accept it. As the years went by, he actually began to find it soothing. Human beings are hard-wired to survive and, subconsciously, Shaun had adapted in order to do just that. Violence was all he had known and there had never been anyone to teach him or show him that there might be a different way. And so he needed to hurt people. We might be tempted to dismiss Shaun's story as extreme or even implausible, but I believe every single word of it. These are lives traumatised in ways and to degrees that are entirely beyond my understanding. These are boys and young men in search of any kind of peace.

On various occasions in the last fifteen years, I have heard it suggested that escalating youth violence ought to be blamed on the lyrics and lifestyles associated with particular genres of music, rap music in particular. But that is lazy thinking, not least given the fact that there are tens of thousands of kids who listen to the same kind of music without ever picking up a blade. It might represent a tempting headline for dull tabloid hacks, but urban music is certainly not the root cause of knife murders in this country. That said, I do recognise the potential for certain songs or performances to act as aggravators – triggers for violence or, at the very least, for an increase in tension between groups and individuals. The same might be said for a range of material posted on the internet or social media. And you can add to that the fact that there is an increasing normalisation of violence in society: in fiction and in fact, on screens and in reality, on the news and on our streets, on a twenty-four-hour rolling cycle. It leads to the very real danger of desensitisation – of a loss of innocence that, with terrifying speed, can become terminal in the lives and deaths of those who know no other way.

Beyond the symptoms and the aggravators, we need to get to the real causes. And the evidence is all there in the child-hoods of those caught up in violence. There is an undeniable pattern to the lives of the knife-crime suspects that I have encountered. The seeds are sown from the very beginning – sometimes as far back as the antenatal months of a boy's life. His mother is being battered senseless before he is even born – he can sense it, he can hear it, he can feel it. And it does him breathtaking harm. His early years are characterised by the continued violence of a broken home. His dad has gone – if he was ever there to begin with – and all too often, the latest boyfriend seems perfectly capable of maintaining the beatings. He sees it all. Sometimes he's a direct target of it. So it becomes all he knows.

When we talk about early intervention with vulnerable children, we are usually referring to work done during primary school years. But in the cases of the boys I have come across, it needs to be much earlier than that. In the most acute cases, it needs to begin as early as conception. The first thousand days of life are everything. The danger is that he will arrive at nursery, aged three, already exhibiting all the signs of trauma; already set on a story without any kind of happy ending. Dead or prison. And we cannot, as a society, stand by wringing our hands and saying that there's nothing we can do.

There are a handful of additional things required for London's long-term plan to work. The first is that it has to be independent of politics. As long as we have politicians (or political appointees) in charge of delivery, the response isn't going to be effective. In my experience, having politicians in charge means that attention spans are short-term – that planning is short-term, that funding is short-term, that action is short-term – and everything is played out along party lines. It means that a Conservative-run Home Office will fail to work effectively with a Labour-run City Hall because both have forgotten that none of this is about them. They have failed to understand that it is all about saving lives.

Knife crime is far too important for politics, and politicians should never be in charge of the plan. But neither should the police be – for two specific reasons. The first is that, with police officers at the wheel, the tendency is to revert to type, to lapse back into short-term, enforcement-led approaches. Because those are the easiest and most familiar things to do. The second is that the relationship between the police and those communities most affected by violence is still characterised by a degree of tension. There is in particular a trust and confidence deficit between the Met and young black Londoners – a group who are disproportionately represented among the victims of knife crime in the capital. According to the *Guardian*, more than 40 per cent of the 132 people murdered in London during the course of 2018 were young men under the age of thirty. The majority of them were the victims of stabbings.[24] Specific data on the ethnicity of victims is harder to come by, but my own review of those 2018 cases would suggest that a significant majority of the young men killed (potentially as many as 75 per cent) came from black and minority ethnic communities.

When I was working with Charlie Howard in Camden, she set up a football match involving some of my officers and some of her young people. Sensitivities were such that the game was nine months in the planning. The boys won, but after the game they refused to eat the cakes that the police had brought for them. This was, in Charlie's words, 'for fear they had been poisoned or bugged'. Some people remain unconvinced that the police are on their side. Policing needs to be at the heart of everything we do in response to knife crime, but not at the head.

The leadership of the twenty-year plan needs to be independent, shared between experienced professionals who know what they're doing and, crucially, young people themselves. Far too often in the past, critical decisions affecting the lives of young people have been taken in their absence. It has got to be different this time. The grown-ups in the room need to give up some of the power and much of the control. Young people cannot be an afterthought; they need to be right in the thick of it, from the very beginning.

*

On 11 December 2017, I attended Parliament to give evidence to the Youth Violence Commission, a community-initiated, cross-party-sponsored inquiry that had been convened to look again at the overwhelming challenges of knife crime and serious youth violence. Karyn McCluskey was there too, sitting directly opposite me on the other side of the room. I talked about the things I had seen and the things that needed to change. I called for a twenty-year plan. In the months that followed, the Commission hosted several more sessions that heard evidence from a wide range of sources, much of it directly from young people themselves.

The Commission shared their findings in an interim report, published in July 2018. The report acknowledged the fact that there are no quick fixes, that any preventative strategy must address root causes and that early intervention is key. It pointed out the link between school exclusion and the propensity for and vulnerability to violence. It highlighted the fact that the relationship between the community and the police is key. It also noted the fact that austerity had made things worse than they would otherwise have been. It drew attention to a 2016 Unison survey of members working in Youth Services, in which 91 per cent of respondents suggested that government cuts were having a particularly adverse impact on young people from poorer backgrounds. In her foreword to the report, Vicky Foxcroft MP, chair of the Commission, wrote that youth violence 'is a national issue. It is also a national shame, because the violence, deaths and injuries are preventable.'

The truth is that we know what needs to be done, it's just that we continue to fail to do it. And the consequence is that the madness of history goes on repeating itself. These are the names of the young people who lost their lives across London in 2018:

1 January – Steve Narvaez-Jara, aged 20, stabbed in Islington

11 January – Harry Uzoka, aged 25, stabbed in Shepherd's Bush

28 January – Yaya Mbye, aged 26, stabbed in Stoke Newington

31 January – Khader Saleh, aged 25, stabbed in Wormwood Scrubs Prison

3 February – Kwabena Nelson, aged 22, stabbed in Tottenham

3 February – Hassan Ozcan, aged 19, stabbed in Barking

11 February – Sabri Chibani, aged 19, stabbed in Streatham

14 February – Promise Nkenda, aged 17, stabbed in Canning Town

18 February – Lewis Blackman, aged 19, stabbed in Kensington

19 February – Rotimi Oshibanjo, aged 26, stabbed in Southall

20 February – Sadiq Mohammed, aged 20, stabbed in Camden

20 February – Abdikarim Hassan, aged 17, stabbed in Camden

5 March – Kelva Smith, aged 20, stabbed in Croydon

8 March – Kelvin Odunuyi, aged 19, shot in Wood Green

14 March – Lyndon Davis, aged 18, stabbed in Chadwell Heath

14 March – Joseph William-Torres, aged 20, shot in Walthamstow

17 March – Russell Jones, aged 23, shot and stabbed in Enfield

20 March – Beniamin Pieknyi, aged 21, stabbed in Stratford

25 March – Abraham Badru, aged 26, shot in Dalston

29 March – Reece Tshoma, aged 23, stabbed in Plumstead

1 April – Devoy Stapleton, aged 20, stabbed in Wandsworth

2 April – Tanesha Melbourne-Blake, aged 17, shot in Tottenham

2 April – Amaan Shakoor, aged 16, shot in Walthamstow

4 April – Israel Ogunsola, aged 18, stabbed in Hackney

16 April – Sami Sidhom, aged 18, stabbed in Forest Gate

21 April – Kwasi Anim-Boadu, aged 20, stabbed in Finsbury Park

5 May – Rhyhiem Ainsworth Barton, aged 17, shot in Kennington

17 May – Abdulrahman Nassor Juma, aged 23, stabbed in Barking

18 May – Osman Shidane, aged 20, stabbed in Ruislip

20 May – Arunesh Thangarajah, aged 28, stabbed in Mitcham

18 June – Joshua Boadu, aged 23, stabbed in Bermondsey

23 June – Jordan Douherty, aged 15, stabbed in Romford

27 June – Ishak Tacine, aged 20, stabbed in Edmonton

12 July – Katrina Makunova, aged 17, stabbed in Camberwell

26 July – Latwaan Griffiths, aged 18, stabbed in Lambeth

1 August – Sidique Kamara, aged 23, stabbed in Camberwell

5 August – Malik Chattun, aged 22, stabbed in Kingston upon Thames

26 August – Shevaun Sorrell, aged 22, stabbed in Deptford

27 August – Abdi Ali, aged 18, stabbed and beaten in Enfield

3 September – Ismail Tanrikulu, aged 22, shot in Tottenham

18 September – Ali Al Har, aged 25, stabbed in Tufnell Park

22 September – Elyon Poku, aged 20, stabbed in Stamford Hill

22 September – Guled Farah, aged 19, shot in Walthamstow

11 October – Hashim Abdalla Ali, aged 22, shot in Hayes

12 October – Moses Mayele, aged 23, stabbed in Hainault

22 October – Ethan Nedd-Bruce, aged 18, shot in Greenwich

1 November – Jay Hughes, aged 15, stabbed in Bellingham

2 November – Malcolm Mide-Madariola, aged 17, stabbed in Clapham

4 November – Ayodeji Habeeb Azeez, aged 22, stabbed in Annerley

5 November – John Ogunjobi, aged 16, stabbed in Tulse Hill

24 November – Zakaria Bukar Sharif Ali, aged 26, stabbed in Dalston

9 December – Aron Walker, aged 18, stabbed in Greenwich

9 December – Jay Sewell, aged 18, stabbed in Greenwich

18 December – Richard Odunze-Dim, aged 20, shot in Edmonton

22 December – Wilham Mendes, aged 25, stabbed in Tottenham

The very least any of us can do is to remember these young people, even if it is only for a moment.

A spokesman for the family of Richard Odunze-Dim – the

year's second-to-last victim – was quoted by the BBC as saying, 'Too many families have gone through the pain that we are going through now. We do not want vengeance, we just want the violence to end.'

*

I want to end this chapter on a note of hope. Because despite everything, I retain a sense of optimism about the lives of the young people caught up in deadly knife and gun crime. And it's not an idle hope; it's one based on experience. I have stood in far too many of the haunted places where boys have been stabbed and lives have been lost, but I have also met and heard the accounts of young men whose lives have been saved, who have turned themselves round in the most extraordinary ways.

At the heart of every one of their stories is the transforming power of relationships – positive, nurturing, loving, life-giving relationships: the very thing that was missing in their old lives. The lost boys with blades and guns have grown up with violence and without fathers; with trauma and lacking any positive male adult role models; with abuse of every kind and without any sort of comfort; with anger as a first and last resort and with no sense of hope or aspiration. What they need more than anything is the friendship and companionship of older women and men who are prepared to remain alongside them, believing in them for as long as it takes until they are able to walk safely on their own. It might be a step-parent or an older cousin. It might be a youth worker or a volunteer on a community mentoring scheme. It might be any one of us. It will almost certainly take years and it will undoubtedly get messy. But it works better than anything else I've come across.

Writing in *The Times* on 3 May 2014, following the involvement of a teenager in the fatal stabbing of a school teacher, my good friend Patrick Regan, then the chief executive of XLP, an urban youth charity working with at-risk young people in some of London's most deprived and challenging neighbourhoods, had this to say: 'Despite the evidence we sometimes see around us, I refuse to believe that this is a lost generation of young people. Change comes through building trusted long-term relationships, sticking with people through thick and thin, re-imagining what they can become.'[25]

Re-imagining what they can become. I like that. As long as they have funding, charities like XLP are in it for the long haul. Their time and effort is spent in developing relationships with the young people they serve, 'loving the hell out of them', as Patrick likes to put it. It is within the context of those loving relationships that young people begin to discover that they have worth and start to realise that their journey needn't end in a mortuary or a prison cell.

VI. *Places of Safety*

'He's Radio Rental,' my colleague whispered.

'He's what?' I replied, a quizzical look on my face.

I was a young PC, early in my probation and still getting to grips with the idiosyncratic language used by some of the more experienced officers I was working alongside. It was a night shift and we had been called to the scene of a burglary.

'Radio Rental... mental... It's rhyming slang.'

The crime had been reported by the occupant of a second-floor apartment in Vincent Square, central London. We climbed the internal stairs and knocked gently on the front door. It was after midnight and we didn't want to wake the neighbours. A middle-aged man opened up and let us in. The first thing I noticed (it would have been impossible not to) was the fact that his flat was almost completely devoid of furniture, but the floor was covered with hundreds of sheets of A4 paper.

As the new lad, I would be expected to write up any subsequent report, so it fell to me to carry out the initial investigation. The scene facing us was undoubtedly odd, but I was beginning to get used to the unexpected. The thing to do was to ask questions.

'Can you tell me what's happened?'

'I've been burgled,' the man replied.

By this time, we had walked through to the main living room. No furniture. Lots of paper. And I could see that all the windows were locked and secured. I reminded myself that we were on the second floor.

'How did the suspects get in?' I asked, as I continued through the flat, looking for a possible point of entry.

'Satellites,' he replied.

That was when my colleague leaned in and whispered to me.

'He's Radio Rental.'

His tone wasn't unkind. It was more matter-of-fact – he'd clearly dealt with this sort of scenario before.

Realising quickly that there had been no actual crime committed, but not wanting to appear rude, I asked another question of the man.

'Who do you think the suspects might be?'

'The FBI.'

'The FBI?' I responded, making a conscious effort to measure my tone. I didn't want to sound immediately disbelieving.

'Yes. The FBI have broken into my home. And they've used satellites to do it.'

The situation was as real to him as he was to me. He believed with absolute certainty that the agents of a foreign government had him under technological surveillance and that they had broken into his flat and stolen things from him. We never got round to establishing what those things might actually be – I tried instead to offer some gentle reassurance, hoping that he felt he was being treated with dignity, before explaining that we would have to leave to deal with our other duties. I wrote the call reference number on a piece of official Metropolitan Police memo paper, and that seemed to satisfy him. I didn't have the heart to tell him that it wasn't an actual crime number – that there would never be an actual crime number.

Back in the control room at Rochester Row police station, we relayed our tale to our teammates, amid the sound of much laughter. He was Radio Rental, we said.

But as I thought about it later that night, I felt uneasy. My dad had suffered all his adult life with bipolar disorder, and so I knew something of the reality and agony of mental illness. Though I had joined in, my laughter was hollow. If the man in the flat was Radio Rental, then so was my dad. If we were laughing at someone who thought he had been burgled by the FBI, we were laughing at my old man too.

As a new police officer in his early twenties, I lacked the maturity or the confidence to say or do anything about the discomfort I felt that day. But in the years that followed, I would go on to encounter more people suffering from mental ill health than I could possibly begin to count: on the street, in police custody suites, at crime scenes (both victims and perpetrators), wandering the corridors of A&E departments, as well as inside their own homes.

The first time I was punched on duty, it was by someone who was mentally unwell. I was working as the operator on Lima 4 – one of the Brixton area cars – and my colleague and I were sent to deal with an 'abandoned call traced' on an estate near the top of Brixton Hill. The female occupant of one of the flats had dialled 999, but the call had been terminated before the operator could get any details. That sort of thing happened a lot, and most of the time it didn't amount to anything. But every now and then the call was abandoned because someone was in serious trouble. And that was the thought you always had in mind as you set off on the blue-light run.

We got to the address in good time and knocked on the front door. We could hear movement inside, but no one answered. As our concern began to grow, I stepped to one side of the door and lifted the letter box using the end of my baton. I had been taught never to put my face directly in front of, or anywhere close to, the opening – you never knew what might come flying through it: bleach or acid; urine or faeces; the blade of a knife. As I peered through the narrow gap from an angle, I could see the figure of a woman standing in the hallway, and it looked as though her hands were covered in blood. I told my colleague what I could see, and within seconds, we had taken the door off its hinges. Section 17 of the Police and Criminal Evidence Act gives a police officer the power to enter a building in order to save a life. And that was exactly what we thought we were doing in this situation – through the front door and into the complete unknown.

As we entered the flat, the woman flew at me, punching me several times in the chest. Though I was wearing body armour and barely felt the blows, we had no option but to restrain her – she was completely out of control. As we tried to work out what was going on, we realised that it wasn't in fact blood on her hands; it was some sort of red modelling clay. And a quick check of the flat confirmed that there wasn't anyone else present. There had been no obvious crime committed before our arrival, but she was clearly very ill. Because she was on private premises, we had no power under Section 136 of the Mental Health Act to detain her and take her to a legally designated place of safety (invariably a hospital or a police station), so we took the decision to arrest her for the assault on me. It felt like the only thing we could do to protect her.

*

During the nineteenth century and the early part of the twentieth, hundreds of thousands of people were detained in asylums: huge Gothic institutions that could be found in every county in the land. Some of the people held in them were genuinely mentally ill, suffering with a broad range of conditions that were not properly understood, even by the leading medical experts of the times, but a significant proportion of them were nothing of the sort. Inmates included those with simple learning difficulties as well as teenage mothers who were considered to be of unsound mind as a consequence of their life choices. And once you had been committed to the asylum, it was almost impossible to leave.

It wasn't until the end of the 1950s (the first modern

Mental Health Act, which provided the first definition of the term 'mental disorder', was passed in Britain in 1959) that the voices of conscience began to be heard, challenging the fundamental inhumanity of this widespread institutionalisation. The beginnings of change began to stir on both sides of the Atlantic. In America, in 1963, President John F. Kennedy said this in a speech:

'Every year nearly 1,500,000 people receive treatment in institutions for the mentally ill and mentally retarded. Most of them are confined and compressed within an antiquated, vastly overcrowded, chain of custodial state institutions... It has troubled our national conscience – but only as a problem unpleasant to mention, easy to postpone, and despairing of solution. The Federal Government, despite the nationwide impact of the problem, has largely left the solution up to the states. The states have depended on custodial hospitals and homes. Many such hospitals and homes have been shamefully understaffed, overcrowded, unpleasant institutions from which death too often provided the only firm hope of release.'

Kennedy proposed a new national mental health programme for the United States and suggested that most patients would be far better cared for within the community. He called for an end to 'traditional methods of treatment which imposed upon the mentally ill a social quarantine, a prolonged or permanent confinement in huge, unhappy mental hospitals where they were out of sight and forgotten'.

The notion of mental healthcare being provided in community settings came increasingly to the fore in Britain during the 1970s, driven in part by a succession of public scandals concerning the appalling treatment of patients in the old Victorian institutions. 'Care in the community' was later adopted as a flagship policy under the Thatcher government of the early 1980s. The Mental Health Act that was passed in 1983 continues to provide the primary legal framework for the assessment and treatment of people suffering from mental ill health in England and Wales.

But for all the good that might have been achieved by this fundamental change in the nature of statutory provision – the closure of the asylums, the beginnings of a greater focus on psychiatric patients as actual human beings – the reality remains that the development of solutions to one set of prob lems actually created a whole host of new ones. While care in the community might be desirable and indeed admirable as a concept, it stands or falls on the basics of funding and delivery. It is one thing to remove the seriously ill from long-term institutional treatment, but quite another to provide the right level of support for them in a community setting.

So much of the experience of front-line police officers during the last thirty years, my own included, has been of standing in the space that exists between those two things – institutional care and community care – dealing with people caught in circumstances where, for any one of endless possible reasons, the notion of care in the community has failed completely. It happens every single day, and on occasions, the consequences are catastrophic.

On 12 May 2011, just after 9 p.m., a man called Badi Salem was murdered in a hostel in Argyle Street, north London. The hostel was a sort of halfway house for people with a history of mental ill health. Badi was stabbed repeatedly and the scene was a particularly gruesome one. I know, because I was on duty that day.

Argyle Street is in Camden, just across the road from King's Cross railway station, and I was the borough commander at the time of the killing. I was working late that day and I heard the call come out on the radio. As soon as I was able, I made my way to the location – not because I thought I would be of much help to anyone, but because I wanted to show my appreciation and support to the first responders who had been confronted with the full horror of it all, to the uniformed officers who would, inevitably, be standing outside on crime-scene cordons for hours on end and to the detectives who had a very long night's work ahead of them.

The suspect – a forty-two-year-old man named Marvin Bailey – was tracked down and captured by officers the day after the murder. Both he and Badi had been residents at the hostel and under the psychiatric care of Camden and Islington NHS Foundation Trust. Shortly before the murder, the two men had been seen by hostel staff talking and sharing a cigarette. There was no apparent indication of what was about to happen.

In December 2011, at the Old Bailey, Marvin Bailey pleaded guilty to manslaughter on the grounds of diminished responsibility. Court-appointed psychiatrists had assessed and diagnosed him as suffering from paranoid schizophrenia.

He had a long history of serious mental ill health, including a tendency towards violent behaviour. The year before the murder, he had been released from the care of a secure psychiatric hospital. An independent investigation into the killing – commissioned by NHS England – identified 'serious shortcomings' in the care and treatment of both Badi and Marvin. The panel report[26] highlighted Marvin's history of violence, his use of drugs and alcohol and his regular failure to comply with psychiatric treatment: 'It seems reasonable to expect that professionals involved with him needed to be alert to the possibility that he might at some point stop taking his medication as prescribed and/or use non-prescribed drugs with a resulting deterioration in his mental state with the risk that he may become violent.' However, the report went on to point out that in the period immediately prior to the murder, there were no specific or obvious signs of what was to come.

Having examined all the available evidence – including the full medical and treatment histories of both men – the panel concluded that the murder was not predictable and, therefore, not preventable. But whether it was deemed predictable or not, the fact remains that a human life had been lost in horrifying circumstances, and that mental ill health was at the heart of it all. The Old Bailey trial judge sentenced Marvin to be detained indefinitely under the Mental Health Act.

It is important to understand that the overwhelming majority of mental health patients are not violent. Most are simply unwell, in the same way that someone with a broken leg or cancer is unwell. And they happen to be some of the most vulnerable people in society, in need of and deserving the best possible medical care. Thankfully, murder scenes of the kind discovered in Argyle Street in 2011 are extremely rare. They are certainly not everyday occurrences, even for front-line police officers. However, there is a broader mental health reality that police officers do encounter every single day, found in the lives and stories of people out on the streets and behind closed doors who have fallen into one of the gaping holes that have appeared in the provision of adequate care – the lack of sufficient hospital beds; the lack of appropriate community-based treatment and support.

For a number of years, I worked as a police hostage and crisis negotiator. It was one of the greatest privileges of my professional life. However, much of my time as a negotiator was spent dealing not with bank robberies gone wrong, but with people suffering from acute mental health crises.

Like the man I met on Hampstead Heath in 2007.

It must have been about one in the morning when the call disturbed me from my sleep. I reached towards my bedside table and, eyes still closed, fumbled instinctively for the handset.

'Hello?' I was speaking in a barely audible whisper. Bear was sleeping next to me and I didn't want to wake her. Our girls were tucked up in their beds and I didn't want to disturb them.

On the line was Sean, a friend and colleague who was on call that night as the Met's negotiator coordinator – the man in charge of any decision to deploy us to an ongoing incident.

I was on his list of negotiators for the week, available for short-notice deployment anywhere in London.

'Can you call me back in two minutes?' I asked. 'I just need to clear my head and get downstairs.'

I rang off and slipped quietly out of bed. I picked up the rucksack sitting by the bedroom door and headed straight down to the kitchen, taking care to avoid the floorboards that creaked. The door clicked shut behind me as I reached for the switch on the wall, my eyes narrowing in the brightness of the sudden light. Inside my rucksack were several layers of warm and waterproof clothing and a child's pencil case containing assorted marker pens, biros and Post-it notes. The simple tools of the trade. I sat down at the kitchen table and selected a pen and a yellow Post-it from my collection. Right on cue, the phone rang again. Sean got straight to the point.

'I need you up on Hampstead Heath. Male threatening to jump into one of the ponds. You'll need to get a fast car run.' He gave me a handful of other details, including the call reference (CAD) number, and told me that he'd meet me there.

Sean hung up and I scrolled through the numbers in my phone to find the one marked CI IR (shorthand for 'chief inspector, information room'), a direct line to the senior officer in charge of the Met's main control room. I got straight through and, having introduced myself, gave him the CAD number. He authorised a traffic car to come and collect me, and I asked for it to meet me at the end of our road.

I knew they would take a few minutes to get there, so I took a shower to make sure I was presentable as well as fully awake, then dressed quickly in jeans, a sweatshirt and a fleece, grabbed the rucksack and headed out into the night.

I heard the sirens before I saw the car. I was holding my warrant card in my right hand as I flagged the marked BMW down with my left. I jumped straight in the back and we were off. The near-deserted streets of south London flashed past as we headed towards the river, and I was alone briefly with my thoughts. How was this one going to play out?

Through Westminster, into Camden, and finally to a car park on the edge of the Heath. Sean had just arrived, and we talked as we walked, picking up the pace as we headed towards the ponds. He provided me with updates based on the little he knew. Local officers had been on scene for a while, talking to a man who seemed intent on jumping into the icy water.

There are not many places in central London that get truly dark, even in the small hours, but Hampstead Heath is one of them. The further we got from the road, the harder it was to see. We picked our way carefully until we found the right place, the silhouettes of uniforms giving the location away. We spoke to the duty inspector and confirmed the plan. It was the same simple one as always: to try to save this man's life.

I walked forward quietly and took up a place beside the PC standing nearest to the pond. About twenty yards in front of us, at the end of what looked like some sort of wooden pontoon, I could just about make out the ghostly figure of a lone man. I listened as he told his story: one of deep sadness that had drawn him in desperation to the water's edge. What can you offer a man who has got to the end of himself? All you have is your kindness, your humanity and your time.

The PC and I listened, we talked quietly, and we waited. And when he was ready, he walked slowly towards us and into the blanket's embrace.

After all these years, I have forgotten his name and the detail of his story. But I haven't forgotten the sense of hope-lessness that ebbed for the briefest moment and enabled him to step back from the edge. He was a very brave man. The air lightened as we left him in the care of local officers and para-medics and made our way back to the car park. Sean offered me a lift home, and an hour or so later, I crawled back into bed as quietly as I had left it, knowing the whisper of peace that always seems to accompany a story with a happy ending.

And yet how happy was the ending for the man on the Heath? I was back home with my family, but what about him? He almost certainly finished the night in a police cell, when he ought to have been in a hospital bed. I suspect he was placed on suicide watch, with a uniformed PC sitting by his open cell door, when he should have been in the care of fully trained and qualified health professionals. And I suspect that he was back out on the streets not too long afterwards, still struggling to access the ongoing support he needed to survive.

I could tell you endless similar stories from my time as a negotiator. There was the Italian man protesting on the roof of a house in west London. It was the middle of a cold winter's afternoon and I needed every layer of clothing I had packed in my bag. The only way to get up to him was with the help of the fire brigade. The only way to speak to him was with the aid of an interpreter. So the brigade brought along one of their mechanical cherry-pickers, and the interpreter and I squeezed ourselves in, alongside a nonplussed firefighter who was required to operate the controls. Once up at roof height, we learned that the man was in dispute with the council about his housing and that he had been unable to persuade anyone to deal with his concerns. This was his last resort, and he was going to jump if his protest came to nothing. Negotiating takes at least twice as long when there's an interpreter involved, but eventually, we were able to reassure him sufficiently for him to agree to come down.

Then there was the man in the communal hallway of a block of flats, holding a kitchen knife in one hand and a meat cleaver in the other. There was the man who had climbed hundreds of feet to the top of a construction site crane and was threatening to jump. There was the man who had covered himself in blue paint and smashed through the roof of a house, hurling tiles into the street below. There was the old man in a sheltered housing block, sitting in an armchair holding a knife to his own throat. There was the man standing on a window ledge less than a foot wide, on the seventeenth floor of a block of north London flats, clinging on by his fingertips. And there was the man barricaded into a flat, seen through a half-open front door, gesticulating wildly with one arm while holding a baby in the other.

Some of the people I met were criminals. Some of them were very dangerous. But most of them were just ill. They ought to have ended up as patients, not as prisoners.

Police officers are dealing with people in significant mental health crisis every single day, and the scale of the challenge is growing all the time. As the desperate consequences of austerity cut deeper, it is the most vulnerable in society who suffer most of all. Mental health provision in this country is wholly inadequate and, in the absence of anyone else, it is police officers who are so often asked to help.

In November 2018, Her Majesty's Inspectorate of Constabulary (HMIC), the oversight body for policing in England and Wales, published a report titled 'Picking up the Pieces'. It had been commissioned to look into police dealings with mental ill health in society, and concluded that the police approach to people with mental health problems was generally supportive, considerate and compassionate, but that too many aspects of the broader mental health system were broken and that it was the police who were being left to pick up the pieces. The report suggested that this represented a failure of care for people suffering with mental illness and was placing an 'intolerable burden' on police officers and staff. It described the whole situation as 'a national crisis'.[27]

There are just 18,000 adult psychiatric inpatient beds in England and Wales. The total rises to about 20,000 when you include those designated for young people. And it is nowhere near sufficient to meet the level of demand that now exists.

In 2014, Paul Netherton, then an assistant chief constable in Devon & Cornwall Police, had taken the unusual step for a senior police officer of using Twitter to describe an example of what the shortage of beds meant in reality. He posted the following series of tweets on the afternoon of Saturday 29 November 2014:

> We have a 16yr old girl suffering from mental health issues held in police custody. There are no beds available in the UK.

> The 16yr old was detained on Thursday night, sectioned Friday lunchtime and still no place of safety available. This can't be right.

> Custody on a Fri & Sat night is no place for a child suffering mental health issues. Nurses being sourced to look after her in custody !?!

The girl was kept in a cell for the best part of forty-eight hours – far longer than police officers would ever be allowed to detain a criminal without charge – for no reason other than that there was nowhere else for her to go. There wasn't a single adolescent mental health bed available anywhere in the UK.

The story made national news headlines, but nothing much seemed to change in the aftermath. Demand continued to outstrip supply, and it wasn't difficult to work out the reasons why. A BBC *Panorama* programme broadcast in February 2017 highlighted the fact that over the course of the preceding four years, government healthcare spending had risen by £8 billion but funding for mental healthcare had fallen by £150 million.

HMIC point out that the Met Police receive a mental-health-related call every four minutes. Officers are deployed to respond every twelve minutes. And in half of all mental health cases where transport is required, it is the police rather than the ambulance service who transport patients to places of safety. The consequent demand on police time and resources is neither justifiable nor sustainable.

Police officers are not trained for this essential work. They are not equipped for it. And they are not resourced for it. The reality is that the system is broken, and it is the seriously ill who are suffering as a consequence. The police service will always be the first agency in line to deal with any form of crisis, and that is exactly as it should be – I have never known a good police officer to turn their back on someone in need of help. And where serious crimes have been committed by those who are mentally unwell, there is no alternative but to arrest and allow the criminal justice process to run its course. But where people are simply unwell, the last place they should ever be taken is to a police station.

If officers are called to a person collapsed in the street and they discover a man suffering a seizure, there would be outrage if they placed the individual concerned in handcuffs and carted him off in the back of a police van. And yet that is exactly what is happening to any number of people who are mentally ill.

*

When I suffered a massive nervous breakdown in April 2013, a police station would have been just about the worst possible place you could have taken me to. But I was one of the fortunate ones. I had a friend who was able to drive me to A&E late on a Friday night, who was willing to sit with me during the interminable wait to be seen that drifted into the small hours. I was registered with a GP who had time to see me on the Monday morning, who recognised what was wrong with me and knew exactly what to do about it. He was more than happy to allow our appointment to overrun for as long as was needed for him to explain, simply and gently, what was happening to me and what he was going to do about it. After the inevitable and agonising wait for its effects to kick in, the antidepressant medication he prescribed for me worked, and has kept on working ever since. He referred me for emergency counselling, and once my six NHS sessions were done, I was able to afford ongoing private therapy that remained necessary for more than five years after I first fell ill. I could do that because I had an employer who continued to pay my full salary for the seven months I was off work due to my illness, and who supported me in working reduced hours on restricted duties when I did finally make it back. I had a group of wonderful friends who visited me and sat with me until I was on my feet again. And most importantly of all, I have an extraordinary wife and family who loved me back to life.

Inevitably, perhaps, I find myself thinking about the people who have none of those things. People who don't have a partner who is able to steady them through the darkest times. People who don't have any kind of place they can call home. People who don't have a job, a salary, sick pay or any other form of financial stability or security. People who can't afford to pay for private counselling. People who don't have a network of friends and colleagues who own cars and have time to sit and listen. People who don't even speak English; who aren't registered with a GP; who have nowhere to turn. People on window ledges and people standing at the water's edge.

Mental health is, of course, a term as wide as life itself, covering a million different conditions, experienced in a million different ways. And the truth is, we still don't really understand it – certainly not to the degree that we understand physical health.

If I were to introduce you to ten different people who had broken their legs, there might be some variation in their stories: one might have been playing football, one might have slipped and fallen at work, one would undoubtedly have been drunk and dancing on a table. There might also be some difference of diagnosis: simple or compound fractures, femur or tibia or fibula or some combination of any of those. And there would almost certainly be a distinction in the specific forms of treatment prescribed: some legs in plaster, some needing pins, some requiring an inflatable boot. But a broken leg is still a broken leg. Most of us understand what that is and most of us understand the basics of what is required to mend it. It helps, of course, that you can see it all on X-rays.

But what about people like me who have broken their heads? If I were to introduce you to ten different people suffering with subtly different forms of mental ill health, where would we begin in trying to understand how to diagnose and treat them? Even the leading experts admit that, the more they understand about the human brain, the more they realise they don't understand. And often people are most afraid of the things they least understand.

As a society, mental ill health scares us. If I am honest, it scares me. The experience of breaking down in 2013 was by far the most terrifying of my entire life. Depression is the relentless, remorseless thief of joy and hope – joy in the present moment and hope for the next. It is, simply, utter darkness. You could offer me all the riches of all the kings who ever lived, and I would never choose to go back there – to the very edge of life. But talking about it helps. In fact, the more I talk about it, and write about it, the less afraid I find I am.

In recent years, there has been the beginning of a much more open and compassionate public conversation about mental health, but we still have a very long way to go in ensuring the provision of appropriate treatment and support for people who are seriously ill. Politicians have begun talking about the notion of 'parity of care' between mental and physical health but, as with so many other things when it comes to politics, those are just empty words in the absence of any real action. There is an urgent need for adequate investment in critical mental healthcare: in the provision of sufficient beds for adults and children alike; in the availability of trained staff to conduct emergency mental health assessments out in the community; in the provision of adequate secure facilities where the dangerous can be detained and treated. There is an urgent need for adequate investment in preventative care too, in early intervention and treatment in the lives of those broken souls who police officers encounter routinely out on the streets. Arguably, the costs to society of the failure to properly treat mental ill health are far greater than the costs would have been to help people stay well in the first place.

But once again, the economic argument pales beside the humanitarian one. If the true measure of a society really can be found in how it treats its most vulnerable members, then we are failing to a spectacular degree.

VII. *Learning to Listen*

Almost two hundred years ago, the then Home Secretary, Sir Robert Peel, set out his vision for policing in Great Britain: 'The police are the public and the public are the police; the police being only members of the public who are paid to give full-time attention to duties which are incumbent on every citizen in the interests of community welfare and existence.'

Peel's view was that officers should be an integral part of the community, working alongside and in relationship with the members of that community. The historian Charles Reith has argued that this approach was 'unique in history and throughout the world, because it derived, not from fear, but almost exclusively from public co-operation with the police'.[28]

This is the prized notion of 'policing by consent', the suggestion that police officers are best able to do their jobs when they enjoy the trust and confidence of the public. But what happens when that relationship is in danger of breaking down completely?

On the evening of 22 April 1993, on the streets of Eltham

in south London, two black teenagers were targeted in an unprovoked racist attack by a gang of white men. The names of the teenagers were Stephen Lawrence and Duwayne Brooks. In his powerful book *Steve and Me*, first published in 2003, Duwayne describes the neighbourhood where it happened: 'Eltham was an infamously racist area. Black people were always getting beaten up round there, and despite two police stations nothing ever got done about it.'

Duwayne and Stephen were close friends. Having spent much of that April afternoon together, they were waiting to catch a bus home when Duwayne spotted a group of white youths approaching them. One of the group, looking in their direction, shouted out, 'What, what, nigger?' and started running towards them, drawing something out from his trousers. Duwayne turned and fled, shouting at Stephen to do the same.

Duwayne managed to escape, but Stephen was caught and stabbed. He died later that night.

The initial police response to Stephen's murder was characterised by a number of substantial shortcomings: in the quality of first-aid training that had been given to officers; in the failure to treat Duwayne as a victim of the attack; in the treatment of Stephen's family on the night of the killing and in the weeks and months that followed; in the conduct of the murder inquiry. Over time, as the full extent of these shortcomings became apparent, the level of public concern about the case grew to such a degree that, in 1998, the Home Secretary, Jack Straw, directed that there should be a full public inquiry into the circumstances of his death and the police investigation that followed. Years later, Straw would suggest that the decision to order the inquiry was the most important he had taken during his time in charge of the Home Office.

The Stephen Lawrence Inquiry report was published in February 1999, and its findings were utterly damning of the Metropolitan Police. The authors of the report accused the Met not only of incompetence and corruption, but of being institutionally racist. Their conclusions rocked the British police service to its Peelian foundations.

As the Met faced up to its undeniable shortcomings and to the overwhelming task of repairing the damage done, talk in the corridors of Scotland Yard turned to how best to begin the process of rebuilding relationships with London's 'hard to reach' communities – those regarded as being most angry with, and alienated from, policing. But from the outset, there was something wrong with the language, and with the mindset that lay behind it. The members of these primarily black and Asian communities weren't hard to reach at all. They lived in the same neighbourhoods as everyone else; they attended the same schools and universities and worked in the same offices and businesses. The only real distinction was that more often than not, they came from the poorer side of the street. Slow realisation prompted a change in the terminology. 'Hard to reach' became 'hard to hear', with differences of language, history, custom and culture suggested as reasons for the ongoing communication difficulties being experienced by the establishment. But that wasn't right either. The labelling – and the thinking – was still wrong. It took time, but eventually policing began to understand. These communities were neither hard to reach nor hard to hear. The truth was that they were simply not listened to. They had been speaking out for years, but most of the rest of us hadn't been paying the slightest bit of attention.

*

I've lived in Brixton in south London for more than twenty-five years. It's my home; it's where my wife and I are raising our children; it's where all three of them went to primary school and where my wife still teaches. We love the place. I suspect that's why I have a particular interest in its history.

At the start of the 1980s, it was just another run-down inner-city neighbourhood, albeit one with a remarkably diverse local population. In the midst of a nationwide recession, growing poverty was matched by rising inequality – between rich and poor; between black and white. Twenty-five per cent of local people were from visible minority ethnic backgrounds, but 65 per cent of those who were unemployed were black. The situation was compounded by the fact that, in keeping with other parts of the country, standards of available social housing were poor, and crime was on the rise.

In 1981, the Met Police responded to a surge in criminality in the Brixton area by introducing Operation Swamp. Large numbers of additional officers were drafted into the neighbourhood, and the controversial 'sus' power was used extensively in an effort to reassert police control of the streets. Dating back to the Vagrancy Act of 1824, sus allowed officers to stop and search anyone considered to be a suspected person, though history suggests it was used disproportionately against young black men. In one six-day period during Operation Swamp, more than a thousand people were searched, and most of them were black. The behaviour of the police served only to exacerbate a growing sense of unease experienced and expressed by members of the local black community, who believed that they were being unjustly targeted. In early April 1981, the atmosphere on the streets was becoming increasingly febrile. On Friday 10 April, a young black man was stabbed. Two police officers came to his assistance and tried to help him into the back of their car. But it would appear that their actions were misinterpreted by a group of passers-by, who assumed that the officers were harassing the young man. They reacted by attacking the vehicle.

The police response was to flood the area with even more officers, but this served only to heighten the tinderbox sense of tension already apparent on the streets. The following day, 11 April, Brixton went up in flames.

Patrick Bishop was a journalist sent by the *Observer* to cover the breaking story. He was accompanied by a photographer named Neil Libbert. Writing in the same newspaper on the thirtieth anniversary of the riots, Patrick described the events of that day.[29] 'I can still recall, with almost psychedelic clarity, the moment that it started – a brick arcing through the air, the crunch of an imploding police van windscreen and the glitter of flying glass in the afternoon sunshine. Shortly after, Brixton was ablaze as roaming mobs vented years of pent-up anger.'

He continued: 'I'd arrived with Neil Libbert that Saturday

morning, sent down from the *Observer*'s newsroom, then in St Andrew's Hill, Blackfriars... The ingredients for an explosion were there and just after 4.30 p.m. it happened. Neil and I were standing in Atlantic Road, near an off-licence, when two very young-looking cops, dressed in jeans and bomber jackets, grabbed a young black man for no obvious reason and announced, in best *Sweeney* style: "You're nicked." As Neil snapped away with his Leica, they bundled the young man towards a police Transit van. It was, as Neil remarked later, "an extraordinarily provocative and stupid thing to do".

During the hours that followed, 279 police officers were injured, as well as at least 45 members of the public. Sixty-one private vehicles and 56 police vehicles were either damaged or destroyed, 145 businesses were damaged, and 82 arrests were made. The following day, a further 122 officers were injured and an additional 165 arrests made.

I have a friend who was raised in and around Brixton in the seventies and eighties. He was a teenager in April 1981, and he was there on the streets when the first missile was thrown. He was witness to much of the chaos and destruction that followed. Talking to me more than three decades later, he offered a powerful insight into what it meant to be young and black in south London at a time when most of the police were racist (at least that was how it seemed to him) and the ever-present threat posed by skinheads and members of the National Front was so serious that he and his friends formed gangs not in order to commit crime, but as an essential means of protecting themselves.

He began by telling me about PC White, a local

community officer who used to patrol the Angell Town Estate in the mid- to late 1970s. 'PC White was different,' he said. 'He wasn't like the others. There was no abuse. He called us by our names.' The simple things done right and well. My friend – and his friends in turn – respected PC White, and so did the community elders. His place in their neighbourhood represented the essence of Peel's vision in action: a relationship between officer and community built on cooperation, not fear. But then, without notice or explanation, PC White was moved to other duties. The local youngsters never saw him again. And everything changed.

The next encounter my friend had with the police came in the form of a passing patrol car that slowed as a uniformed officer wound the window down and shouted a single word at him: 'Coon!' And so the police were confirmed as the enemy, to be feared and never to be trusted. PC White had evidently been the exception, not the rule.

But the 1981 riots were ignited by more than just police racism and their misuse of search powers, significant though those things were. The reality – and the lived experience – ran much deeper than that. In my friend's view, the fundamental causes of the disorder were societal and systemic, and they had been building up for years: overwhelming inequality and disadvantage reinforcing the marginalisation and isolation of large sections of the black community in Britain's most challenging neighbourhoods. Young black men were more likely to be turned over by the police, but they were also more likely to be poor, unemployed and living in the places where crime was high and aspirations were low. My friend asked me a simple question: 'How are we ever going to get justice from a system that is, fundamentally, unjust?'

I would never seek to absolve criminals of their evident guilt, but I do believe that we have a responsibility to try to understand the reasons why the riots happened.

In 1981, Home Secretary William Whitelaw asked the respected barrister and judge Lord Scarman to carry out an urgent inquiry into the events that had led to the most serious disorder seen on the streets of Britain in the post-war years. His report was published in November 1981, by which time there had been further disturbances elsewhere, notably in Liverpool and Manchester.

Scarman identified a series of 'complex political, social and economic factors' that had created a 'disposition towards violent protest' and called for 'urgent action' to address the racial disadvantage that was 'no doubt... a fact of British life'. He also set out a series of concerns specific to policing, not least high levels of community mistrust and a loss of confidence in policing methods that were apparent in so many local neighbourhoods. Interestingly, and in stark contrast to the later findings of the Lawrence Inquiry, he stated that he did not believe the Met Police were institutionally racist.

His report was the catalyst for significant change – in policing at least. The 1984 Police and Criminal Evidence Act (PACE) is probably the most important piece of law enforcement legislation to have been enacted in my lifetime. It had direct consequences for stop and search, for the making of arrests, for the detention and treatment of prisoners and for the identification and interview of suspects.

And it introduced the requirement for police officers to have 'reasonable grounds' before they could search or arrest anyone. The days of sus were over.

Other Scarman legacies included the formation of the Police Complaints Authority – an independent body charged with investigating public complaints about police conduct – and the establishment of police and community consultative groups (PCCGs) – local forums for community members to hold local police officers to account. And while elements of PACE have evolved over time, and the various labels afforded to complaints and consultation provisions have changed, Scarman's recommendations have, in broad terms, stood the test of time.

That said, back in the 1980s, the publication of his report didn't mark the end of all troubles. Far from it, in fact.

On Saturday 28 September 1985, Met Police officers launched an armed raid at an address in Brixton. They were searching for a suspect named Michael Groce, who was wanted for questioning in relation to alleged firearms offences. But the operation went dreadfully wrong when Michael's mother, a black woman named Cherry Groce, was shot by one of the officers who had entered her home. She survived, but sustained life-changing injuries that resulted in her being paralysed from the waist down and remaining wheelchair-bound for the rest of her life.

The incident led directly to two days of serious disorder on the same London streets that had experienced the riots of 1981. Two hundred arrests were made and more than fifty people were injured. A few days later, a press photographer named David Hodge died of an aneurysm, having apparently been attacked by a group of looters he was taking pictures of.

Following her eventual death in 2011, a post-mortem examination found that Ms Groce had died of kidney failure, linked by the pathologist to her original gunshot wounds. In July 2014, an inquest jury highlighted a series of police failings that had contributed to her death. In response to these findings, the then Commissioner of the Met, Sir Bernard Hogan-Howe, issued a public statement and an 'unreserved apology'. He accepted that the police operation on the day of the shooting was inadequate in both its planning and delivery.

But he was speaking three years after Ms Groce had died and almost thirty years after the original raid. I suspect that it's not just her family who were left wondering why on earth it had taken so long.

A week after the shooting of Cherry Groce, four police officers searched the north London home of another black woman, Cynthia Jarrett. They had arrested her son earlier the same day and stated that they were looking for stolen property. But during the search, Ms Jarrett collapsed and died of a heart attack. The following day, members of her family met with the local police and demanded an inquiry into the circumstances of her death. Despite the anger they must have felt, they made it clear that they did not want to see any disorder on the streets. But their pleas went unheeded.

That evening, officers were attacked with missiles and petrol bombs. Cars were overturned and torched, while shops and other buildings were set ablaze. In response, five hundred police officers were deployed onto the streets around the Broadwater Farm Estate. Among their number was a constable called Keith Blakelock.

Just before 10 p.m., reports came through that several gunshots had been fired. One officer had been hit and seriously injured. Half an hour later, Keith was dead. He and his colleagues had been trying to protect members of the London Fire Brigade who were responding to a blaze in one of the blocks. As officers and firefighters alike were forced to retreat, Keith tripped and fell. He was surrounded by a mob and hacked to death. The cowards actually tried to behead him. I have listened to recordings of police radio transmissions made during the last moments of Keith's life. The horror of what happened that night is beyond my capacity to understand or explain.

The riots in Brixton in 1981 and in Brixton, Tottenham and beyond in 1985 all happened in deprived inner-city areas that were home to significant minority ethnic populations. But who or what was to blame?

Two of Prime Minister Margaret Thatcher's policy advisers, Oliver Letwin and Hartley Booth, had no doubt where responsibility for the disorder lay. They co-wrote a briefing paper suggesting that neither poverty nor racism had played any part. Rather, they suggested that the causes were to be found in the choices and actions of lawless individuals: 'Riots, criminality and social disintegration are caused solely by individual characters and attitudes. So long as bad moral attitudes remain, all efforts to improve the inner cities will founder.'

Two government ministers of the time – David Young and Kenneth Baker – had put forward a series of proposals designed to tackle the poor state of urban housing and to encourage black entrepreneurship, but Letwin and Booth dismissed their suggestions: 'David Young's new entrepreneurs will set up in the disco and drug trade; Kenneth Baker's refurbished council blocks will decay through vandalism combined with neglect; and people will graduate from temporary training or employment programmes into unemployment or crime.'[30]

When the briefing was made public in 2015, Mr Letwin was compelled to apologise 'unreservedly' for what he had written. In suggesting that poverty and racism had played no part in causing the unrest, he and his colleague had displayed a casual and cynical kind of prejudice that I suspect was far from unique among those in power during the 1980s. The revealed content of the Letwin/Booth document doubtless came as no surprise to members of the black community, with their first-hand experience of serious discrimination, played out repeatedly through the generations. The repetition of the past is certainly one of the reasons why the shooting of Cherry Groce and the death of Cynthia Jarrett – and the riots that followed both – continue to have such a prominent and powerful place in London's history.

*

The story of police–community relations during the last thirty years is punctuated by the names of black men and women who have died during police operations, in the back of police vans or in the isolation of police cells. The nationwide riots of 2011 were triggered by the fatal police shooting of a black man named Mark Duggan. Some individuals, Duggan included, were suspected of involvement in very serious crimes, but none of them deserved to die. The circumstances of some of the deaths remain unexplained, at least to the satisfaction of relatives and friends, who continue to demand answers from the police, the Home Office and the Independent Office for Police Complaints.

While the frequent truth is that there was no conspiracy or cover-up – or even culpability – on the part of the police, that is unlikely to be so in every case. It is both understandable and entirely appropriate therefore that we continue to ask searching and sometimes deeply uncomfortable questions about deaths in police custody – or 'deaths following police contact', as they are sometimes known. And when those inevitable questions come, the first and most important requirement of those in positions of authority is to listen.

*

One of the key Met initiatives in the months immediately following the Stephen Lawrence Inquiry was the development of what was termed 'independent advice'. Outspoken critics of the Met were invited into the heart of the organisation and offered a seat at the table. And it wasn't a cynical case of keeping your friends close and your enemies closer; the intention was much more constructive than that. Advisers were asked to review and comment on everything from organisational policy and strategy to the conduct of individual murder investigations. It represented a massive culture change for the force, and in the early days the idea was not without its opponents. But my experience and that of so many of my colleagues during the years that followed could not have been more clear: every time we paused to listen to the voices of those we served, and determined to act on the basis of what we had learned, we ended up doing a better job than would otherwise have been possible.

In November 2000, the year after the Lawrence Inquiry report was published, a young black boy named Damilola Taylor was killed on the streets of Peckham in south London. It happened ten days before his eleventh birthday and his story horrified the nation. He was walking home from the library at the end of the school day when he encountered a group of other children on a local housing estate. Half an hour later, he was dead, the consequence of a severed artery in his left thigh. Several years later, two brothers were convicted of his manslaughter.

As a detective inspector based at the Racial and Violent Crime Task Force (RAVCTF), I was asked to attend a series of gold group meetings held in the days immediately following Damilola's death. Gold groups were a relatively recent development – chaired by the police but attended by independent advisers, community leaders and local authority partners. This was new and different territory: inviting members of the public into confidential briefings to hear sensitive operational details disclosed by a senior investigating officer (SIO), to discuss police strategies and tactics and to make recommendations about what might happen next. At the RAVCTF, we had been instrumental in the introduction and development of gold groups, and in those early days we were frequently called upon to offer guidance and advice.

I remember taking my place for the first time in the conference room at Southwark police station. As the area commander sat down at the head of the table, none of us was in any doubt about the seriousness and significance of the case. The commander opened proceedings and asked us all to introduce ourselves. There were two independent advisers in the room – both black women with strong local ties – and they had been invited to be there from the very start. There was no secret meeting-before-the-meeting that they had been excluded from. Everything I heard, they heard too. We listened to the SIO in charge of the case, to the local superintendent responsible for community policing, to representatives of various local government departments and then to the advisers themselves. And, of course, they wanted exactly what everyone else wanted: justice for a little boy and his stricken family. With their help, we considered the particular needs of the investigation, of Damilola's family and of the wider community. By working with them, by allowing them to ask awkward, difficult questions, by listening to them and learning from them, we became more effective. These days, independent advice is a fairly routine part of any major investigation. Back then, it felt like a revolution.

*

The police need the community and the community needs the police. It seems to me that one of the most basic requirements for good community relations is good community policing: local officers who are known by local people (not least those who may not have much faith in the Met as an institution but who nonetheless believe in 'their' local PCs), who understand the history of a place, who know where the villains live and which streets to patrol, who know when something is out of place and who are trusted to do their jobs well. One of the most positive and popular developments during my entire time in the Met was the introduction in 2004 of local Safer Neighbourhoods teams (SNTs). I was there with the Commissioner, standing on a north London housing estate alongside the Prime Minister and the Mayor of London, on the day of the SNT press launch.

London has more than six hundred local authority wards, and under the Safer Neighbourhoods programme, every single one of them was given its own dedicated community policing team, consisting of a minimum of one sergeant, two PCs and three police community support officers (PCSOs). It represented a huge investment of resources, and the promise to communities was that these officers would not be taken away to perform other duties and would consequently be able to devote their time and attention to long-term local problem-solving. Over time, the hard work of the teams and their community partners – not just in London, but in many other parts of the country too – had a transformative effect. I don't think it's any coincidence that, around the country, there were some very significant reductions in crime in the decade that followed the widespread introduction of dedicated neighbourhood teams.

Community policing has rarely been regarded as the headline-grabbing bit of the job. For the most part, it doesn't tend to involve car chases and bank robberies and armed sieges. But it might just be the bit of policing that makes the greatest difference to the real lives of real people. It might also be the part of policing that has the greatest impact on the levels of confidence and trust that ordinary folk have in the work the police do. So much of the job is about empathy and rapport. If you trust me, you are more likely to talk to me. If I listen to you, I am more likely to understand what needs to be done. If we work together, between us we might just make some sort of a difference in the streets where I work and you live.

But community policing requires the kind of sustained investment that is now in very short supply. The truth is that neighbourhood teams throughout England and Wales have been decimated by austerity. The loss of more than 20,000 police officers in England and Wales between 2010 and 2018 meant that something had to give. Many things, in fact. In most parts of the country, neighbourhood policing has effectively ceased to exist. In London, SNTs are a thing of the past. And, entirely unsurprisingly, crime is now rising.

More than a decade ago, I sat in a briefing at Scotland Yard, listening as an assistant commissioner (AC) introduced us to something he called 'the Neighbourhood Policing Re-invention Cycle'. There were four stages, and from memory, they looked something like this:

Stage 1
Falling crime
Falling public concern about crime

Stage 2
Falling political concern about crime as an election issue
Falling investment in neighbourhood policing

Stage 3
Rising crime
Rising public concern about crime

Stage 4
Rising political concern about crime as an election issue
Rising investment in neighbourhood policing

By the end of Stage 4, we were all the way back round to the beginning. The AC was able to demonstrate a direct correlation between levels of investment in neighbourhood policing and levels of recorded crime. But it would appear the politicians weren't paying the slightest bit of attention.

Those who fail to learn from the past have always been destined to repeat it. The loss of dedicated neighbourhood policing in so many parts of the country – as a direct and undeniable consequence of austerity – has done significant harm to local communities. And it will take years – perhaps even generations – to repair. While the harm is perhaps most evident in the crime figures, it is also apparent in the strain placed on police–community relations. It is incredibly difficult for local people to form trusting connections with police officers they rarely see and whose names they do not know. Equally, as crime rises and demand rises and the calls just keep on coming, it becomes increasingly difficult for police officers to pause for long enough to listen to the voices and the stories, the fears and the concerns of the people they serve.

And listening is everything.

*

Before I was ever deployed as a hostage negotiator, I had to apply to become one. Having passed the initial paper sift and subsequent interview, I got through to the final stage: the practical assessment. So it was that early one morning in the late spring of 2005, I took the Underground to Colindale in north London.

Arriving at the detective training school, I made my way upstairs to the second floor, where I was greeted by a member of staff from the Met's permanent hostage unit. I was given a short, simple briefing and directed towards a closed door at one end of a deserted, strip-lit corridor. I was informed that behind it was an unknown colleague playing the part of an officer who hadn't shown up for work that day. No one knew the reasons why, but his team were worried about him. I was given his name and told that this was his home address.

I decided straight away that the best approach was to treat the scenario as though it was entirely real. Standing to one side of the door, I called out to him. Voice not too loud; I didn't want to startle him.

Silence.

I paused for a moment, before calling again. This time, I introduced myself and explained that I was concerned about him and wanted to know if there was anything I could do to help. There was the sound of shuffling feet on the other side of the door.

'Who is it?'

His voice was soft and sad. I repeated my gentle introduction and asked if he would be willing to open the door and talk to me. No, he said, he would prefer to keep things just as they were. I was left with no alternative but to begin trying to communicate with a man I could not see, whose face and life I did not know. I realised later on – once the exercise was over – that the door was never going to open. That wasn't the purpose of the assessment. You might be forgiven for thinking that police negotiators are selected on the basis of their talent for talking, for persuading – perhaps for their ability to solve seemingly intractable problems. But that isn't it. Talking is important, of course, but what the team from the Yard really wanted to know was whether I could listen. To words that are spoken and those that are not. To subtle notes and changes in tone: hints of hope or weariness, of resolve or remorse, of determination or resignation. To the sounds that are beyond words: gut-deep groans and whispered sighs; sharply drawn breaths and puff-cheeked despair; wry laughter and held-back tears. And to the poignant, laden silences that fall between words. Standing alone in the corridor, I began to listen, and there, in his words and among his words, were all the clues I needed to unlock his story.

I made it through the assessment and, later that year, took my place on the fabled training course: two weeks of incredibly long hours and sometimes overwhelming emotional intensity that were designed to prepare us for the real world. In the years that followed, I was called out countless times. Often to the middle of nowhere, frequently in the middle of the night. Always to someone in trouble. And in those places I learned, time and time again, that listening can save lives.

VIII. *Keeping the Peace*

I used to love public order training – or riot training, as it was more commonly known. The Met had its own large, purpose-built site (originally in Hounslow, now in Gravesend), complete with a private network of streets, buildings and alleyways where we could work our way through a series of testing operational scenarios under fairly realistic conditions. We would be based there for forty-eight hours at a time, working late into the evening on the first day to give us experience of dealing with disorder that might occur under the cover of darkness. As with so many things in policing, we were training for events that every decent, law-abiding citizen hopes will never happen.

The first day always began with the infamous shield run. Shortly after arriving on site, we would get changed into our full kit: flame-proof overalls, arm and shin guards, body armour, kit belt, gloves, steel-toed boots and visored helmet. After the warm-up, everyone assembled on the start line, each of us holding a long shield. Made of Perspex, the shields were almost 1.7 metres in length (taller than some of the officers carrying them) and weighed just under 6.5 kilograms. We were expected to carry them as we ran the full distance of the course, and there was an inevitable sense of relief when we had finished and everyone had made it round inside the allotted time.

With the run complete, it was time for the fun to begin – at least, it was fun for as long as it remained within the comparative safety of a secure training environment. Facing disorder for real is an entirely different proposition. We were taught a series of shield tactics and techniques and shown how to put them into practice on the streets and in the alleys of the training estate. Instructors played the part of rioters and they didn't hold back. The bricks they threw at us might have been made of wood, but the petrol bombs were real. Every police officer who has done the training can recall the *whump* of heat and flame as the first one lands at your feet. We were taught how to take junctions, how to hold streets and how to deal with sudden attacks that came from behind us. And we learned that it was all about working as a team.

For the final act on the second day, we were joined by our Mounted Branch colleagues and their beautiful, powerful horses. In full flow, they were a magnificent sight to behold. We would take it in turns to play the bad guys, facing them from a distance of about fifty yards, pelting horses and riders alike with tennis balls. Then the order would be given for them to charge, and from the first twitch of the first horse you knew it was time to get out of the way as fast as your legs could carry you. As they thundered past us, the only thought was one of gratitude – that out in the real world, if order really were to break down, they would be on our side.

In the early part of my career, the need to draw on the specific public order skills taught at Hounslow were comparatively rare. The majority of the major events I dealt with were largely peaceful in nature. Occasions like the Changing of the Guard and Trooping the Colour are part of the rhythm and routine of London life, ceremonial and solemn and splendid. My role was frequently no more than to provide a source of visible reassurance, to maintain public safety and to keep the traffic moving. In the early 1990s, we were still faced with the very real threat to the mainland posed by the IRA, but even they tended to avoid planting bombs in places that put large numbers of civilians at risk.

I can still recall my first Remembrance Sunday on duty, a bitterly cold November day in 1993. I was part of a team of officers assigned to a long line of fixed posts on Birdcage Walk. For hours on end, I stood alone in a uniform that was designed for neither warmth nor comfort. I was wearing a long-sleeved shirt, a tunic and a raincoat so useless that the wind just whistled straight through it. I'm not sure that I've ever been so cold in my life, either before or since. My freezing circumstances were redeemed only by the fact that I happened to be standing outside the back of a rather smart central London hotel. The staff in the kitchen must have seen me and taken pity on me, because one of them appeared next to me with a steaming mug of hot, sugary tea. I wasn't a tea drinker by habit, but I wrapped my hands around the cup and savoured every last sip.

When I think of all the great national celebrations that have happened in my lifetime – royal birthdays, weddings and jubilees; official state visits; Olympic parades; the return of the World Cup-winning England rugby team – I think of the police officers lining the streets, quiet and steady and unobtrusive. Sharing a joke with the family in the front row, maintaining the Queen's peace. Standing by, just in case. And it isn't just the celebrations. I remember the thousands who gathered along the Mall in the days following the death of Princess Diana. I was working nights that week and spent an entire shift walking silently among the mourners camped out at the side of the road.

Wherever you find a crowd, you are almost certain to find a police officer.

The Notting Hill Carnival, a flamboyant fixture of west London life since the late 1960s, is one of those major public get-togethers that divides popular opinion. For most people, it is a spectacular celebration of African-Caribbean culture and history, the largest and most significant of its kind in Europe. For many, though – and in spite of the evident best intentions of organisers and the vast majority of participants – there is the concern that, each August Bank Holiday week-end, it provides cover for the actions of a small minority of dangerous criminals, frequently made plain in the form of serious violence.

In my early years as a PC and a sergeant, carnival was regarded primarily as the source of enormous amounts of overtime, with a minimum of sixteen hours worked on both the Sunday and the Monday. And we were paid double time for the second day – the bank holiday itself – which meant that I was able to earn more than a full week's additional wages in the space of just forty-eight hours. My role was as part of a small public safety team responsible for patrolling the entirety of the carnival route and looking for places where the size and movement of the crowds (to say nothing of the levels of alcohol consumption) might be starting to put people at risk of getting hurt. We would identify 'pinch points' – such as the railway bridge outside Westbourne Park Tube station, where vast numbers of people were funnelled from a comparatively wide street into a much more confined area – and radio them in to carnival control, giving the people in charge an opportunity to implement contingency plans.

The carnival area was split into sectors, each under the command of a senior officer known as the sector 'bronze'. If we on the safety team identified the potential for crowd crushing in Sector 1, it would be the responsibility of Bronze 1 to take action to address it. He or she would implement a clearance plan – often relying on the assistance of police horses – to relieve the congestion. So far, so good. But almost straight away, we identified a further dilemma. In many cases, the act of relieving the crowd pressure in one place served only to create a new crushing problem further along the route – in a different sector, under the command of a different senior officer. I saw it with my own eyes: Sector 1 might have been fine, but Sector 2 was now in trouble. And it taught me something significant that remained with me for the rest of my policing career: solving your problem by creating a problem for someone else really isn't solving anything at all.

It's a powerful lesson that has so many possible applications. For much of my career, for instance, individual London boroughs were in competition with one another to see who could achieve the best reductions in crime. But all too often, the act of target-setting simply drove perverse behaviour. Rather than invest in effective long-term crime reduction work, individual boroughs would simply go to great lengths to displace criminality (and the criminals responsible for it) over the border into the borough next door. It was nonsensical common practice for years.

The same observation might also be made about the relationships that persist between some statutory partners – local authorities, probation services, youth offending services and so on – who have a dreadful habit of passing unresolved problems (usually in the form of actual human beings) from one agency to the next. The immense challenges involved in dealing with a repeat offender who has complex personal needs can be far too easy to palm off on the next unwitting professional in line. The scenario might begin with the Youth Offending Service (YOS), who discover that their teenage subject is living in a home where he is at risk of exposure to violence or some other form of abuse. So the file is passed to Social Services, who already know about the family, but who identify the fact that the young person in question has developed a problematic drug habit. They pass the file to the Drug Treatment Service, who then suggest that the boy has an undiagnosed mental health problem and that until this is addressed, no other form of intervention is likely to work. While he is waiting to be assessed by Child and Adolescent Mental Health Services (CAMHS), the boy turns eighteen, and his new-found adult status means that overall responsibility for what happens to him passes from the YOS to the Probation Service.

So the grim merry-go-round continues until he is reported as a high-risk missing person and, at 4.30 p.m. on a Friday afternoon – the point at which many statutory agencies seem to pack up for the weekend – the police are called and the responsibility for everything is passed to them. At no point in this process does anyone seem to have asked what is best for a person who might well be a violent criminal but who is also a deeply vulnerable young adult. It just seems easier to hand him on to the next agency, in the knowledge that you can at least strike him off your own case list. But the stubborn truth remains that solving your own problem by creating one for someone else isn't solving anything at all.

It was the crowds at the Notting Hill carnival who taught me that.

Notting Hill was also the scene of one of the first major armed incidents I was involved in. It happened in the middle of one carnival Sunday afternoon, when reports came through that an officer had seen someone standing at the window of a first-floor flat holding a gun. The superintendent in charge of that sector of carnival immediately co-opted me – a relatively young and inexperienced sergeant – as his loggist, and I was given responsibility for documenting his decisions, his rationale and the police actions that followed.

The situation could hardly have been more challenging. We were surrounded by tens of thousands of people, midway through the largest, loudest street party you're ever likely to see this side of Rio or New Orleans. The roads and pavements were absolutely jammed, and while the building he was in had been identified, the suspect and his intentions were completely unknown. If he were to open fire on the police or the wider crowd, then in addition to the prospect of multiple gunshot wounds, we were facing the likelihood of a panicked stampede of people and the certain catastrophe that would follow. Everything was at stake.

I listened intently as urgent, hushed discussions took place among the people in charge, as maps and plans were spread out on car bonnets and various alternative scenarios were debated and dismissed. There was nothing else for it: we were going to have to go in. There was no way we could leave an armed man on the loose in the middle of the main carnival area. Or anywhere else for that matter. And any attempt at prior evacuation of the crowd was liable to spread precisely the kind of panic we were trying so hard to avoid, to say nothing of the possibility that it might provoke the suspect to start shooting. Decisions like these are taken in fast time, on the basis of whatever information is available (irrespective of how incomplete it might be) and without the benefit of any of the hindsight relied upon by the 'nine o'clock jury', who, when things go wrong, convene without fail the following morning to pass judgement on actions taken by the men and women who are actually in the arena.

I watched as armoured Land Rovers full of firearms

officers made their way through the crowds. Progress was painfully slow, as they did their best to give the impression that everything they were doing was perfectly routine, that there was no cause for alarm. I stood by as final plans were drawn up for an armed entry to the target address. I grabbed a drink for the hostage negotiator who arrived at the scene, having been called out in anticipation of a possible siege situation developing. There was tension all around me.

As the firearms officers took up their prearranged positions, the call went out for complete radio silence. All transmissions were forbidden until the team had gained entry and secured the suspect. So we waited, none of us saying a single word. We were listening intently for the sound of the gunshots we hoped would never be fired. By him or by us. We were waiting for a murmuration in the crowd – a sudden surge, a massed change of direction that would be the consequence of things going badly wrong – praying that none would materialise.

Continued radio silence. They must have got through the communal door. Surely they were up the stairs and ready to go in. Then a whispered voice crackled through the quiet:

'We've done the wrong door.'

It would have been comical had it not been so serious. Silence again as the armed team regrouped and went a second time. This time, they were successful.

'Suspect detained. No shots fired.'

Thank God for that. I found out subsequently that the firearm in question was an imitation, but it's impossible to know that for sure until the weapon is physically in the hands of experienced officers trained to know the difference. When they went through that front door (on both occasions), the armed team had no idea that the gun was a fake. They were prepared to risk their lives for the sake of a crowd of total strangers dancing in the streets below.

As everyone stood down, we caught our breath. All around us thousands of laughing, swaying, smiling revellers continued on their way, oblivious to the events of that afternoon. And to what might have been. On average in England and Wales, police firearms teams are deployed about 14,000 times a year. On average, they actually discharge their weapons on just four to six occasions.

*

Large crowds are always capable of taking on an unexpected life of their own – moving in a series of collective ebbs and flows that bear no relation to the wishes or intentions of any individual among them. I saw it at Notting Hill, as people were swept along in a particular direction, irrespective of whether or not they actually wanted to go that way. Some were practically lifted off their feet and carried with the tide, and in that moment, there was nothing they or anyone else could do about it. I have seen the same in Trafalgar Square on New Year's Eve and at any number of major football matches.

At the football, it's not just the movement of the crowd that can take you by surprise; it's also the collective behaviour of its members. But while the movement can sometimes be involuntary, the behaviour is always a choice. On occasions, it can be a thing of beauty – I have stood as a supporter at

Anfield, the home of Liverpool FC, on the night of a European semi-final and experienced a sound and an atmosphere unequalled in sport – but all too often, it is anything but. Manchester United fans sing about the death of Liverpool fans at Hillsborough. Liverpool fans sing about the death of Manchester United players at Munich. Black players are taunted with monkey chants and gay fans dare not fly the rainbow. Emboldened by numbers and afforded the supposed anonymity of the horde, football supporters – almost uniquely among sports spectators – are capable of saying and doing things that have no place in any kind of tolerant, civilised society. In a spectacular display of hypocrisy, a significant proportion of them would never dream of behaving in that way apart from the crowd. It is the crowd that makes it possible.

And invariably, it is the police who are charged with fixing the problem. A few years back, I took my place in the match commander's chair at Craven Cottage, the home of Fulham FC. As the contest was played out in front of us, I divided my gaze between the pitch and the crowd. Fulham were always a pleasure to police. Back then, they were the only club in the Premier League not to have a recognised hooligan group among their supporters. There was very rarely any trouble at their ground, and if there was, it was never the home fans who were responsible. Fulham won a corner just in front of the away end, and as one of their midfield players prepared to take it, I saw him flinch. He stepped back from the ball and put his hand up to his face. It was immediately obvious that he had been hit by something thrown from the crowd.

He appeared to brush the incident off, evidently just wanting to get on with the game, but I sent a couple of my officers down to the TV truck to review any available camera footage and try to identify the source of the missile. Despite the full cooperation of the TV company, we were unable to find the person responsible. They were hidden in the crowd. After the match was over, I went to check on the injured player and saw the large welt that was swelling up millimetres below his left eye. He had been hit by a coin. While my colleague took photographs of the injury, I found myself wondering at the behaviour of an anonymous fool who might so easily have cost a man his sight and his career.

A few years later, I was on duty for a Champions League match at the Emirates Stadium, home to Arsenal FC. I had been joined by a senior officer from another force who wanted to observe the police operation at a European game. As the ninety minutes got under way, I showed him round the stadium, and we ended up standing just in front of the away supporters. Without any warning, I was hit full in the face by a bottle of water thrown from the crowd. I suppose I ought to have been grateful that the cap was still screwed on and that it didn't contain something really unpleasant, but that wasn't actually my first thought as my head rocked suddenly backwards. The bottle was full and had been thrown with some force. But as had been the case at Fulham, the offender was lost in the masses.

Sometimes the football problem is far greater than the challenge presented by an isolated idiot throwing bottles or coins. I was a child of the 1970s. I grew up with recurring newspaper and TV images of football hooligans running wild in stadiums and on the streets. I experienced it first-hand. I remember my dad taking me to an Arsenal game when I was about six or seven. They were playing Manchester United at Highbury, and after the match, large numbers of rival fans started knocking lumps out of one another. I was utterly terrified, hiding under the wing of my dad's coat as we made our way onto the Tube platform while the fighting raged all around us. And I remember the huge man who approached us, holding a glass bottle in his left hand. 'Don't worry,' he said. 'I'll look after you.' Though we had some cause to be grateful to him, the situation was one of complete madness – the manifestation of what became known to many as 'the English disease': unchecked racism and bigotry, relentless tribal aggression and serious violence.

Fans had to be segregated from one another, fences were built, and, finally, English clubs were banned from European competitions as a consequence of supporter behaviour, most infamously at Heysel. On 29 May 1985, Liverpool met Juventus in the final of the European Cup. It was supposed to be a celebration of football, involving two of the finest teams on the planet, and I had been allowed to stay up late on a school night to watch it on TV. But before the match even started, serious disorder broke out between the two sets of fans. In the desperate minutes that followed, during which a large section of stadium wall collapsed, thirty-nine people were killed and six hundred others were injured. The authorities went ahead and played the game – perhaps not fully appreciating the scale of the disaster – but football no longer mattered that night. I turned off the TV and went to bed, horrified and bewildered, wondering what had become of the beautiful game.

By the time I joined the Met in the early 1990s, the football situation had improved somewhat. The violence was less frequent, the hooligan groups less evident. But there was always the potential for it to rear its head. In 1995, serious crowd trouble broke out at an international match played between England and Ireland at Lansdowne Road. In 1996, following England's semi-final elimination from Euro 96 at the hands of Germany, there was significant disorder in Trafalgar Square.

Over the course of my career, I policed games at Wembley, Chelsea, Fulham, Queens Park Rangers and Arsenal. For all the scuffling and stupidity I encountered, I never had to deal with any full-blown rioting among fans. But some of my colleagues were less fortunate.

In 2002, Birmingham City beat Millwall in an important end-of-season match, played at Millwall's stadium in southeast London. Fighting broke out in the streets surrounding the ground immediately after the game, resulting in injuries to forty-seven police officers and twenty-four police horses. Sergeant Russell Lamb – a highly experienced public order officer – was among the injured. A BBC News report from the time quoted him as saying that the streets were 'like a battlefield', with fellow officers 'dropping like ninepins'. He described two hours of 'ridiculous, mindless violence' and suggested that it was 'one of the most frightening situations' he had ever been involved in.[31] Seven years later, Millwall lost a match at West Ham and trouble flared both inside and outside the stadium. One fan was stabbed and twenty others were injured.

Millwall supporters have a reputation as bad as any in England. But is the violence problem unique to them? Or is it a broader football issue? Many have argued that it goes much further than that – that it is evidence of a wider societal malaise; that football is the context, but not the cause. As I write, it is evident that football continues to have its troubles, not least with allegations of ongoing racism among the supporters of certain clubs. A BBC News report published in September 2019 stated that hate crime at football matches in England and Wales had risen by 47 per cent during the previous season.[32] And this would appear to be coinciding with the conspicuous and troubling re-emergence of the far right – a consequence of events far beyond sport, but finding voice and expression within the swell of the crowd.

When it comes to the largest displays of civil disaffection, London is usually the destination of choice. It is a city on the world stage and the nation's capital, home to Parliament and the Prime Minister and to the headquarters of the biggest names in international commerce. And the fact that it is also the main operating base for most of the mainstream national media is particularly helpful if you want to maximise the chances of getting your face and your cause onto the rolling news bulletins or the front pages of the following day's papers. You might begin with a rally in Hyde Park, home to Speakers' Corner. Then march in numbers through the heart of town, down Park Lane and Piccadilly into Trafalgar Square and on to Whitehall, passing the entrance of Downing Street before gathering outside the Palace of Westminster to exercise your democratic right to protest – your basic human right to freedom of opinion and expression.

The responsibility of the police when the crowds gather in this way is to facilitate lawful protest, though never to tolerate the actions of those who would choose to break the law. Officers line routes and escort marchers and guard premises that might be targeted by demonstrators. They close roads and direct traffic and do their best to keep the rest of London moving. On occasions, they find themselves standing in the spaces between rival factions, who trade insults and accusations, and who would surely trade blows were the officers not present. When I joined the Met, part of the oath I took was to 'cause the peace to be kept and preserved' to the best of my power and ability. It was the same promise we all made.

It mattered not what my views might be about the causes of those who marched. I was a Crown servant, prohibited by regulations from engaging in any form of political protest or campaign. Privately, I might have been in complete agreement with the concerns of those present – ironic, given the fact that many of them would have regarded me as the enemy, simply by virtue of the uniform I wore. Or I might have wanted to make clear that I stood opposed to everything they represented, not least in their evident hatred of those who were not like them. But the job of a police officer is to remain apart, dispassionate, defending the right of people to say what they have to say, even if they disagree with every word and sentiment expressed. Noam Chomsky, the US academic, writer and philosopher, once suggested that 'if we don't believe in free expression for people we despise, we don't believe in it at all'.

Yet freedom of speech is not freedom to riot. Those who assert their right to protest must also accept their responsibility to do so peacefully. I believe that there is such a thing as an unjust law, and I hope I would be brave enough to take part in acts of civil disobedience if faced with circumstances of overwhelming injustice. But I also hope that, in doing so, I would follow the example of some of the greatest heroes of history – Gandhi and Rosa Parks and Martin Luther King among them – who believed that protest must always be non-violent.

On Saturday 31 March 1990, a little over two years before I joined the Met, thousands of people gathered in central London to protest against the deeply resented poll tax. The tax had been introduced by the Conservative government of the day, and critics suggested that it favoured the rich at the expense of the poor. Protesters met first in Kennington Park, south of the Thames, but by early afternoon an estimated crowd of 200,000 people had converged on Whitehall and Trafalgar Square. I remember vividly watching the news bulletins that were broadcast later that evening, showing scenes of complete anarchy unfolding in the heart of London: missiles flying, police lines buckling and horses charging. And I'll never forget the footage of the lone police car that drove unwittingly into Trafalgar Square before being surrounded by the mob, and watching as a metal scaffolding pole was rammed through the driver's window while he tried desperately to get clear. It was a miracle he wasn't killed. All around the West End, buildings were damaged or set on fire. More than a hundred people were injured and more than three hundred arrests were made. I share the view that the poll tax was unjust, but I also take the view that the actions of those who resorted to violence and other forms of serious criminality were without justification.

The first serious disorder of my career happened in October 1993, in south-east London, when an anti-racism march descended into a riot. The protest had been organised by the Anti-Nazi League and others to demand the closure of a bookshop that served as the headquarters of the far-right British National Party. The shop had opened in Welling in 1989 and the local area had seen a significant increase in racist attacks in the months and years that followed: Stephen Lawrence was murdered in neighbouring Eltham in April 1993. Several thousand protesters gathered in Plumstead and marched to the Welling area, but part of their intended route – the section that passed immediately in front of the bookshop – was blocked by the police, who doubtless feared that it would be damaged or destroyed by the crowd. And therein lies some of the rub. Though I may despise the BNP and all they stand for, I am still bound by duty and law to protect what's theirs. Police attempts to divert the march were met with a violent response, and in the disorder that followed, seventy-four people were injured, including twelve police officers.

I remember the day well. I was working my regular shift

in central London, but the disturbances were serious enough for the Met to activate its force mobilisation plan, meaning that each division was asked to make officers available for urgent deployment south of the river. I was still in my probation and hadn't completed my riot training yet, but evidently they decided to send as many of us as possible to support the officers on the ground. In the event, by the time we actually got there, the fighting was done. But I haven't forgotten the eerie silence of the deserted streets and the bricks and debris that littered the ground as far as I could see. Like some old harbour town in the wake of a great storm.

In September 2004, the Countryside Alliance arranged a large demonstration to protest against government proposals to ban fox hunting. Thousands of people descended on central London to make their voices heard. I was a public order commander by this point in my career – a uniformed inspector leading a team of twenty-four riot-trained officers – and we were assigned the role of mobile reserve. I don't think anyone was expecting trouble – these were respectable folk from rural communities after all – but we were there just in case. We were on standby in Parliament Square when reports came through of clashes between officers and demonstrators in streets close by. We were advised of intelligence suggesting that some of the protesters were planning to storm the Houses of Parliament, and were told it was our job to make sure that didn't happen. We were instructed to kit up. My team (or 'serial', to give them their proper name) was joined by one or two others, and we lined our vans up across the full width of the road and pavement in front of the main entrance to the House of Commons. Then we took our places in the narrow gaps between the vehicles, shields up, visors down. At the time, I didn't hold any particularly strong personal views about fox hunting, but I was very clear what I thought about people trying to break into Parliament. The briefing I gave to my officers was one of the shortest and simplest of my career:

'They will not get through.'

Like Gandalf before the Balrog. We were the last line and I was determined that we would hold it. The crowd charged at us, but none of them got through. I learned later that during the demonstration, forty-eight of my colleagues had been injured – some with broken bones – in addition to a number of members of the public. The then Commissioner, Sir John Stevens, admitted that the disorder had taken the Met by surprise. He also confirmed that the force would identify lessons to be learned from the events of the day and that they would examine the actions of individual officers to see whether any had overreacted in their treatment of protesters. And that is exactly as it should be, because the police don't always get it right. On occasions, whether individually or collectively, they get it terribly wrong. The death of Ian Tomlinson during the G20 protests of 2009 represents a particularly grim reminder of just how badly things can end.

Public order situations are, by definition, chaotic, and it is inevitable that mistakes will sometimes be made. The police service must never shy away from admitting to them and learning from them and doing everything it can to avoid their repetition in the future. At the same time, there should be no hiding place for police officers who resort to any form of violence that cannot be justified. I promised to keep the peace, but I also promised to keep the law.

When lawless minorities hijack legitimate causes to provide cover for their behaviour, the already challenging role of the police in large-scale public order situations is made significantly more difficult. I will defend with my last breath your right to protest: about human rights, about foreign wars, about basic poverty, about government policy, about state visits by the leaders of totalitarian regimes, about austerity, about any of the myriad things that matter to you. Now that I am retired, I might even line up alongside you. And I will defend your right to challenge the police to be better at what they do, to act with restraint and to say sorry when they get things wrong. Indeed, I will join you in making that challenge. But I will never defend violence or criminality of any kind. Those are the very things that render a just cause lifeless.

*

The riots of 2011, sparked by the fatal police shooting of Mark Duggan, began in Tottenham, but quickly spread to other parts of London and beyond. I hope I have some understanding of the fundamental concerns of those who want to ask questions about the circumstances in which black men die at the hands of the police – indeed, about the police treatment of black men in general. I hope I recognise the significance of the levels of mistrust in the police that persist within some communities. I hope I am able to empathise with those who believe that they have been asking the same questions and raising the same concerns seemingly for years without ever feeling that they have been given anything approaching a satisfactory answer. Some of them will say that, unless there is violence on the streets, nothing will ever change. But that wasn't the view of Dr King or the Mahatma and I am with them. There has to be a different way.

The sheer scale and extent of the disorder in 2011 sent shock waves through government and wider society and provoked an unequivocal reaction. Politicians were quick to condemn and police chiefs were swift to promise action. The rioters were pursued immediately and relentlessly, they were named and shamed on the front pages of the national press and they had the book thrown at them by the courts. I was part of the police response and I understand the sense of anger and urgency that lay behind it: my borough was one of those undone by violence and devastation; my colleagues had been out there risking their lives. So we nailed the suspects with the bricks and the bottles. Then we refused them bail. They went to jail, directly to jail, and their feet barely touched the ground.

There is no doubt in my mind that they deserved to face the consequences of their actions, but I would not be the only one to reflect on the way in which the establishment dealt with them and compare it with the treatment given, for example, to the bankers who were held responsible for the staggering financial crash that had occurred three years earlier. In a series of deliberate acts, one group of individuals had set a number of buildings on fire, at a cost of millions of pounds. But it might also be argued that, in a series of equally deliberate acts, the second group had set the entire UK economy on fire, at a cost of billions of pounds. After the riots, the prosecutions came faster than you could count them, but in the years that followed the banking crisis, it appeared that, almost without exception, the guilty were going to get away with it. Writing for the Channel 4 website in September 2011, the journalist Jon Snow articulated what many were thinking: 'In one month, hundreds of rioters and looters have been prosecuted and punished by the English courts, often for offences with a value of under fifty pounds. Yet the threat to the well-being of UK plc was far greater from the bankers than from any number of more arrestable rioters.'[33]

While the rioters saw out their time in jail, the bankers appeared to slip back into the shadows, bailed out by the state – by the taxpayer; by you and me. Whether or not you agree with that reading of events, what cannot be denied is the searing sense of injustice felt by those who believe that, while all men and women are made equal, some appear to be more equal than others: one rule for the powerful, one for the plebs. And it is precisely that sense of injustice that causes people to take to the streets in the first place.

*

At the time of writing, there has been no widespread serious disorder in Britain since the summer of 2011. But all is not entirely well on the streets. The years following the 2016 referendum on Great Britain's membership of the European Union have ushered in a whole new era of public protest, with every new Brexit announcement greeted by a fresh wave of demonstrations and counter-demonstrations. On one side of Parliament Square, pro-European protesters gather beneath their blue and gold flags, interrupting live news broadcasts and demanding a fresh 'people's vote' to determine whether or not we should retain membership of the EU. On the other side, Leave campaigners wave Union Jacks, interrupting the same bulletins and demanding instead that we respect the 'will of the people' expressed in the original referendum result. And while most protests have been peaceful and the majority of protesters have stayed on the right side of the law, that has not always been the case. And there can be no future guarantees. The government's own contingency plans, drawn up in the event of Britain leaving the EU without a deal, make specific mention of the potential for serious disorder on the streets. It is no short-term concern: the deep societal divisions caused by Brexit are likely to remain for years to come.

All this comes at a time when policing in this country is under pressure as never before, due primarily to a combination of rising crime and the crippling long-term consequences of austerity. Each new public march or demonstration demands a further abstraction from already scarce police resources. Frequently, these happen at very short notice, leaving fewer officers available to get on with the day job – dealing with knife crime and domestic violence and all the rest.

In the face of it all, the blue line is being stretched more thinly than ever before.

IX. *The Rise of Extremism*

On Wednesday 22 March 2017, PC Will Johnson was working 7 a.m.–7 p.m. as the operator on Trojan 417, one of the armed response vehicles (ARVs) tasked with responding to firearms related calls in central London. The first half of the shift had been uneventful: the morning briefing, followed by designated patrols, punctuated only by a brief stop for a brew. They were back at their Lambeth base – just across the river from the Palace of Westminster – for a proper meal break when the first call came out. Will hadn't actually managed to eat anything when his radio burst into life.

'Shots fired... Houses of Parliament.'

He remembers the instant hurtle – officers taking stairs three or four at a time in the flat-out run to get to the cars. He and his crew were first through the back gates. They didn't have many details, but none of them was in any doubt about the seriousness of the situation.

Out of the base and onto Lambeth Road. Across the roundabout and onto Lambeth Bridge at incredible speed, the driver picking his way expertly through the traffic. Will ran through a swift check of his kit, the muzzle of his carbine resting between his boots in the front passenger footwell of the car. They were so close, there was very little time to think. Right onto Millbank. A few hundred yards and closing, into the unknown. He saw people running towards them, away from Parliament Square, looking scared.

They screamed to a stop outside the ornate gates leading into Palace Yard, the front wheel hitting the kerb hard. It was utter chaos. On the Lambeth radio link, south of the river, they were dealing with what they believed was a serious road traffic collision (RTC) on Westminster Bridge. On the Westminster radio link, north of the river, they were managing an armed incident at Parliament. As they scrambled out of their car, Will and his crewmates were oblivious to the connection between those two things. Two more ARVs pulled up right behind them and a team of highly trained police officers went to work. They were still operating on the basis of exceptionally limited information. They knew there had been an attack, but they had no idea how many suspects were involved. They thought it was at least two.

As Will ran into Palace Yard, he could see immediately that there were two men lying on the ground. The one furthest from him was surrounded by a large number of people, and at first, Will wasn't aware that he was a police officer. But he could see that there was medic kit scattered everywhere. The man lying closest to him only had a couple of people with him, and in those first few seconds, Will had no idea that he was the suspect. In fact, his first thought was that he might have been a delivery driver, caught up in the attack. Instinct and experience kicked in.

As he made a swift check of his immediate surroundings, he heard the reassuring sound of his armed colleagues shouting, 'Cover's on!' and felt able to lower his own weapon and rush to the aid of the man on the ground. His only thought was to try to save this stranger's life. Gloves on, he started to cut the man's clothing away, and that was when realisation began to dawn. The casualty being tended to a few feet away was in fact one of his own, PC Keith Palmer. The man lying motionless in front of him was a terrorist.

Will found himself in a place that few have ever been, that few could ever begin to imagine. He felt immediately conflicted. He remembers a sense of revulsion, the realisation that he was faced with the worst that humanity is capable of. But he also knew that he had a job to do. His responsibility was to try to save the life of an extremist – perhaps, one day, to put him before the courts and allow them to decide on questions of guilt and judgement. He started on chest compressions, recognising very quickly that his task was almost certainly hopeless. Then, recalling that hearing is the last of the senses to fade, he told the terrorist that he was under arrest for murder. Perhaps that was the last thing the man ever heard. More likely, though, he was already gone.

Adrenalin rattling through him, Will understood that he was in the midst of something huge. He remembers the air ambulance landing in the middle of Parliament Square and the orange-boiler-suited medics running straight to Keith's aid. But by then he knew it was too late. Keith's killer was dead too, and without pause Will joined his colleagues in conducting an emergency armed search of the Houses of Parliament. They still believed that there was a second suspect at large, and weapons drawn, moving at speed, they completed a full search of the area, never knowing what lay round each new corner. Always knowing that there was an officer down in Palace Yard.

Talking about these events almost two years later, Will could remember it all in pinpoint detail. It was obvious that he still wrestled with the fact that he had given CPR to a man who had taken the life of one of his colleagues. He wondered how Keith Palmer's family might feel about his actions. He wondered how he would feel if he was in their place. And yet he knew that he had done what needed to be done, what any one of his colleagues would have done – what Keith himself would have done. It was a case of who was on duty at the time and who was closest by, and that day it just happened to be him. He hadn't seen it all through the filtered lens of a television camera or the carefully edited content of a newspaper report. He'd seen it all with his own eyes. And his story reinforces for me something that is extraordinary about policing in this country. Even in the most extreme of circumstances, the first instinct is never to kill; it is always to save lives. Even the life of a murderer.

Later on the evening of the attack, still dressed in full uniform, Will found himself standing in a queue at a takeaway in Waterloo. He hadn't eaten since breakfast, and despite everything, he was hungry. He remembers being surrounded by members of the public, glued to their phones, reading and watching the news, oblivious to the part that the officer standing next to them had played in the tale being told.

*

When I first joined the police in the early 1990s, the notion of a suicide attack on UK soil was inconceivable. Back then, it was the IRA who represented the primary terrorist threat to the British mainland.

Growing up in the 1970s and 1980s, I was accustomed to grim headlines about the latest IRA atrocity. In October 1981, terrorists planted a bomb at a burger bar in Oxford Street that killed the Met Police explosives officer who was attempting to defuse it. In July 1982, they detonated bombs at military events in Hyde Park and Regent's Park, murdering eleven soldiers. I remember the grainy news footage showing the large tarpaulins covering the bodies of dead horses. In December 1983, an IRA car bomb exploded outside Harrods. Six people, including four police officers, were killed and ninety members of the public were injured. Then, in October 1984, during the Conservative Party annual conference, they bombed the Grand Hotel in Brighton. Five people died, though the Prime Minister and senior members of her cabinet survived. I can still see the TV pictures broadcast from the front of the hotel, the building part-collapsed as emergency services personnel worked desperately to get to those trapped inside. I can still see the MP Norman Tebbit lying on a stretcher, dressed in his blue pyjamas, being lifted slowly out of the rubble, his face caked with dust and creased with pain. The IRA claimed responsibility for the attack in a statement issued the following day, which contained these chilling words: 'Today we were unlucky, but remember we only have to be lucky once. You will have to be lucky always.'

In July 1990, the Conservative Member of Parliament Ian Gow was murdered by a bomb placed by the IRA beneath his car outside the family home in East Sussex. Several years later, as a serving officer attending a training course, I was shown a series of evidential photographs taken at the scene. They remain among the most horrifying images I have seen in my life. Seared into the back of my brain, they disturb me even now. I cannot even begin to imagine how it must have been for my colleagues who were on duty that day, tending to a desperately disfigured dying man.

There seemed to be no end to the terror. I remember the 1991 mortar attack on Downing Street and the 1992 Baltic Exchange bombing. By the time of the latter, I had passed selection for the Met and was waiting for my start date. When I began at Hendon, the reality of the threat was drummed into us repeatedly. In the evenings, after classes had finished, we would take turns to patrol the training school car parks, checking each vehicle to ensure that it was authorised to be there.

In the early hours of 14 November 1992, just two months into my recruit training, PC Raymond Hall and PC Gary Angove carried out a routine traffic stop on a lorry in Stoke Newington, north-east London. Without realising it, they had stumbled across an IRA active service unit planning to detonate a bomb larger than the one that had devastated the Baltic Exchange. The lorry contained more than three tons of high explosive. Two suspects decamped from the vehicle's cab and the officers immediately gave chase, oblivious to the seriousness of the situation they were facing. PC Hall, a former soldier who had served in the Falklands, managed to catch up with the two men, whereupon one of them pulled out a handgun and pointed it directly at the officer's face. Instinctively, PC Hall ducked and the bullet fired by the suspect grazed the top of his skull. Then, as the unarmed officer tried to find cover, he was shot in the back. The following year, Patrick Kelly was sentenced to twenty-five years in prison for his part in the bomb plot and for the attempted murder of PC Hall.

I don't know whether the shooting of a police officer gave my mum and dad any cause for alarm. I don't know whether they were troubled by the realisation that their son was about to start patrolling the streets of the city where it had happened. If they did have any concerns, they certainly didn't mention them to me. And I didn't give it a second thought: I couldn't wait for the adventure to begin.

I finished my training at Hendon in February 1993 and my first posting was to Rochester Row in central London. The Houses of Parliament, Downing Street and Buckingham Palace were all within a short walk of the station, which meant that much of my early time as a PC was spent on dedicated counter-terrorism security patrols. It was me and my colleagues with our wooden sticks, chain-link handcuffs and crackly old Storno radios against the IRA. In truth, the patrols were mind-numbingly boring – hours spent walking alone in streets where nothing ever seemed to happen. But they were an unavoidable necessity, and who knows what we prevented just by being there.

Despite the significant levels of police activity, the main-land attacks kept on coming, and not just in London. In March 1993, the IRA murdered two children and injured more than fifty other people in an attack carried out in Warrington. The following month, they bombed Bishopsgate in central London. The police received a coded warning, but the evacuations were still under way when the device went off. More than forty people were hurt, and one journalist was murdered. The cost of the damage caused was later esti-mated at £350 million. In 1996, an attack on Canary Wharf in London's Docklands killed two more people and caused millions of pounds of further damage. On and on and on it went, all the way through to the latter part of the 1990s. It was only in 1998, with the signing of the Good Friday Agreement, that an alternative to armed struggle became a realistic possibility.

In the years that followed, the dissident Irish Republican threat never went away completely, but it was overtaken in both significance and scale by the growing spectre of inter-national terrorism. And on 11 September 2001, everything changed.

I was on holiday with Bear and her family when it hap-pened. It was the year before we got married. We sat together in disbelief as we watched news footage of the planes hitting, rolling for hours on a constant loop. This was a new kind of terror: indiscriminate attacks designed specifically to cause mass civilian casualties, driven by twisted religious ideology and perpetrated by those who were willing to die for their cause.

In the summer of 2005, it was Britain's turn. On Wednesday 6 July, London celebrated winning its bid to host the 2012 Olympic Games. I can still recall the sense of unbridled joy, the realisation that the greatest show on earth was coming to my home town. But the very next day, all of that was forgotten as four suicide bombers detonated devices on Tube trains at Aldgate, Russell Square and Edgware Road, and on a bus in Tavistock Square. Fifty-two people were murdered and hundreds more were injured on a day of infamy.

I was on duty when the bombs exploded, but nowhere near the scenes of devastation. The duty of climbing into smoke- and dust-filled carriages and onto that splintered bus belonged to the police officers, firefighters, medics and members of the public who happened to be closest by when the explosions happened. And I am in awe of the humanity and heroism they displayed that morning.

In the days that followed, I found myself briefing officers under my command about a kind of threat that none of us had ever encountered before – not in our part of the world at least. It would be easy, with the passing of time, to forget how London felt in those days immediately following the attacks. The city was on edge and anxious, its inhabitants struggling to comprehend what had happened. And yet there was a sense of defiance too, a refusal to give in to terror. Within days, ordinary people were putting on T-shirts bearing the London Underground logo and printed with the words 'We are not afraid'.

Two weeks later, on 21 July, it almost happened again. Four more bombers, three more Tube trains, one more bus. The detonators fired, but they failed to ignite the main charges. This time I was very close by – just a few hundred yards from the smoking rucksack abandoned on the platform at Shepherds Bush Green as the suspect made off down the tracks. I ran to the scene and joined my colleagues in a race to get the cordons in place. The rest of the day became a blur that saw the beginnings of a huge manhunt for four terrorists who were on the run. They were caught eventually, but not before Jean Charles de Menezes had been shot dead by police at Stockwell Underground station, having been mistaken for one of the suspects.

Throughout the latter part of July, all our operational effort and attention was concentrated on catching the killers and preventing further attacks. But there was also a pressing need to offer reassurance to the people of London, not least to members of local Muslim communities who, while wanting to distance themselves from the beliefs and actions of extremists, feared that they might be subjected to revenge attacks carried out by people who held them – or their religion – responsible for what had taken place.

The first time I visited the Parsons Green Islamic Centre was in the immediate aftermath of 7/7. Tucked away in a quiet back street just off the Fulham Road, it was an important local hub for the Muslim community, and as the chief inspector in charge of neighbourhood policing in the area, it was my responsibility to go and talk to its members about the attacks. I arrived there early one evening with a list of important messages that I needed to pass on, but unsure of the reception I might get. I was shown to a packed upstairs room, where I was met by dozens of enquiring faces, all staring intently at me as I took my place at the front. None of them was remotely hostile. None of them expressed any form of resentment at my being there. Understandably, many of them were feeling anxious, but mostly there was just a shared sense of the seriousness of the situation. I spoke about the events of the preceding days, about the need for vigilance within local communities and about the urgency of identifying any intelligence concerning possible future attacks. I gave them a number to call if they had any information to pass on and reassured them that they could speak to the police in absolute confidence if they had any fears or concerns, not least about the potential for crimes to be committed against members of their own families. I told them that the police were there for them as much as they were for anyone else.

Then it was time to listen. There was a great deal they wanted to ask and say, but one thing in particular stayed with me on the short walk back to the station later that evening. They told me that the police only ever came to see them when something was wrong: in the aftermath of an atrocity, or when faced with the threat of one. The implication was that in every other circumstance, we simply ignored them. And I had to admit to myself that there was some truth in what they were saying. After all, it wasn't until something unspeakable had happened that I'd first called by.

I made the decision then that I was going to start visiting them on days when nothing was wrong. Precisely *because* nothing was wrong. In the months that followed, I began to

get to know Abdul, one of the centre's management committee members. We would meet without any sort of agenda,
just to spend time listening to one another, learning from
one another, building a relationship. We talked about life and
family, about faith and the wider concerns of the world. He
would introduce me to a verse or a teaching from the Koran
and I would do my best to respond with something from the
Bible. And I came to appreciate just how much we shared –
as men, as husbands and fathers, as citizens and as pilgrims.
I was enriched by knowing him.

By the time of the next terrorist attack in London, I was
working in a different part of the capital. But I know that,
had I still been based in Fulham and duty had called me
to the Parsons Green Islamic Centre, I would have been
welcomed at the door by my friend.

As I look back on the summer of 2005, I'm conscious of the
questions that continue to come up, not least the one asking
how we ended up living in a world where suicide bombers
rode the London Underground. Did the causes lie in the
complexities of geopolitics, in centuries of history or in the
widespread fallout from wars? Was man-made and man-
twisted religion to blame, or did it simply come down to the
individual choices of wicked human beings?

A few years back, I had the unusual privilege of spending
time in the company of a convicted – and reformed – terrorist. I'll call him Sami. Years before, he had planned to become
a mass murderer just like the men of 9/11 and 7/7, and he
had spent a number of years in prison as a consequence of

his role in a major terror plot. But by the time I met him, he was a changed man. There are plenty of people willing to talk about radicalisation, but not very many with Sami's kind of first-hand lived experience. And there are still fewer able to offer hope that descent into extremism need not be a one-way ride. Over the course of a number of conversations, he told me a little of his story.

He was born in Britain to devout Muslim parents and struggled endlessly with the combination of religious and cultural pressures that characterised his childhood. Over time, his relationship with his family broke down and he moved to London. A young man, rootless and drifting, he fell under the spell of the preachers of hate. He had learned the Koran by heart by the time he was eleven years old, but any beliefs he might have held were undermined by men who taught a desperately distorted version of Islam. And steadily, he lost his mind. He told me about the years he spent in Afghanistan, attending terrorist training camps, meeting the most senior members of al-Qaeda, being drawn in ever deeper. He described the moment he accepted his suicide mission, recalling the AQ commander's embrace. He later came back to Britain, bringing with him the explosives he intended to use to take the lives of hundreds of people.

He returned to his family home and a subsequent conversation with his father. His parents knew where he had been, though they didn't know what he had done or what he had in mind to do. But they left him in no doubt about their views. If it turned out that he was a 'sleeper' (a terrorist lying low, waiting for the right moment to attack), his father told him that he would kill him. And that conversation was the trigger for a change of heart and the beginnings of a change of mind. Sami made the decision not to go ahead with his attack. Eventually, the authorities caught up with him and found the hidden explosives. He offered his full cooperation to the police, he served his time, and you might now describe him as an anti-extremist. His life and journey came full circle.

In all the time I spent with Sami, he never once tried to justify what he did, and he never shied away from accepting responsibility for his actions. His hope was that others might be able to learn from his experience. The overwhelming pressures of culture and religion had driven him to the edge. The loss of any sense of place in the world and the malevolent influence of godless men had pushed him over it.

The late politician Tessa Jowell described radicalisation as 'a response to hopelessness'. Perhaps that's what it is: the messed-up result of a messed-up life; the search for a cause to believe in or a place to call home. I think it is also, in part, a response to rage – a deep anger felt in the face of perceived injustice that finds no other means of expression. Fascinatingly (and alarmingly), some of the potential triggers for extremism are similar to those experienced by the young people who end up in criminal gangs: broken family relationships, exclusion from education or from wider society, basic poverty and inequality, the search for meaning and belonging. Those are precisely the vulnerabilities that preachers of hate and extremist recruiters seek to prey on.

Whatever the complex combination of causes in each

individual case, the threat of radicalisation remains a clear and present danger in Western society. And increasingly, the method of attack has moved away from the sophistication of explosives (the Manchester Arena bombing being an obvious exception) and towards lower-tech, harder-to-detect means. In many of this country's most recent cases, the terrorists' weapons of choice have been vehicles and knives – think of the murder of Fusilier Lee Rigby and the attacks on Westminster and London Bridge. It's illegal to possess explosives and it's a dangerous business making bombs. But there are no such difficulties when it comes to hiring a car or opening the kitchen drawer.

*

When I first returned to work after my illness in 2013, I was offered a behind-the-scenes role at SO15, the anti-terrorist branch. I wasn't fit for operational duties – it was many months before I could even manage a basic five-day week – but there were simple back-office duties that I was able to perform. While I was there, I had the opportunity to hear one of SO15's most senior officers speaking about his growing concerns about the impact of the war in Syria.

With its origins in the so-called Arab Spring of 2011, the Syrian conflict offers a compelling illustration of the truth that global events have local consequences. It quickly became apparent that a war happening almost three thousand miles away had enormous significance for the counter-terrorism effort in the UK. News bulletins carried numerous stories of radicalised British nationals travelling to Turkey, then crossing the border into Syria to participate in jihad. Once there, they were trained in the use of weapons and explosives and hardened in battle. Some of them were killed, but many survived to make the journey back to Britain. And the fact was that these returning fighters were infinitely more dangerous to the security of the country than they had been on the day they first left. But it wasn't just those with first-hand experience of the war. Like Iraq and Afghanistan before it, the Syrian conflict yielded endless stories and images that could be used online to radicalise a whole new generation of the disaffected. My senior colleague believed that the adverse consequences of Syria would continue to be felt in the UK for at least a decade after the fighting had first begun. Experience is proving him right.

But for all the implications of battles being fought in the Middle East, it is important to recognise the fact that twenty-first-century British terrorism is not the sole preserve of the Islamists.

I am writing this book amid deeply troubling signs of the re-emergence of far-right extremism in Britain. Some would doubtless argue that it never really went away.

Back in April 1999, the terrorist David Copeland attacked members of London's black, Bangladeshi and gay communities. His weapons of choice were home-made bombs, each containing hundreds of four-inch nails.

On Saturday 17 April, the first bomb, apparently targeting the black community, went off in Electric Avenue, Brixton. Forty-eight people were injured, many of them seriously. The following Saturday, a second device went off in Brick Lane, east London, an area that is home to a large Bangladeshi community. Thirteen people were injured. The final device, planted in the Admiral Duncan pub in Soho, in the heart of London's gay community, went off on the evening of Friday 30 April. Three people were killed and many more were seriously injured, including three who lost limbs.

I remember the Brixton bomb with particular clarity. The device went off just outside the Iceland supermarket that I walk past every time I head to or from the Tube station. I have seen the CCTV footage of the blast – the sudden detonation and the thick cloud of smoke and dust that enveloped the entire street. The fact that no one was killed is a miracle, particularly when you realise that the bag containing the device was picked up and moved by a member of the public on more than one occasion before it went off. It could have been me who was injured. It might have been a member of my family or one of my closest friends. As it was, those who were injured were people I lived alongside. And an attack on any one of us was an attack on all of us.

At the Old Bailey, Copeland was given six life sentences for three murders and three counts of causing explosions. While accepting that he was mentally ill, the court had refused to accept his plea of manslaughter on the grounds of diminished responsibility. As the trial proceedings drew to a close, the judge said this to him:

'Anyone who has heard the facts of this case will be appalled and horrified at the atrocity of your crimes. The evidence shows you were motivated by virulent hatred and pitiless contempt for other people. You set out to kill, maim and terrorise the community. As a result of your wicked intentions you have left three families bereaved. You alone are accountable for ruining their lives. Nothing can excuse or justify the evil you have done.'

Gary Reid, who lost a leg in the Admiral Duncan blast, spoke out after the trial had ended:

'The fear, loathing, hatred and ignorance culminating in the bombings is a warning to society and the world as a whole that racism, prejudice and homophobia – and the fear of difference – is out there. We should all be aware of this and challenge it at every opportunity.'

Copeland suggested to investigating officers that had he not been captured, he would have carried out further attacks. He had at one point been a member of the British National Party, and evidence points to his having had links to other far-right interests and organisations.

That was 1999, but the evidence of more recent history is every bit as concerning.

Just after midnight on Monday 19 June 2017, a suspect in a hired van drove into a group of worshippers close to Finsbury Park mosque in north London. It was not long after the end of prayers. One man was killed, and a number of others were injured. The driver of the van was a man called Darren Osborne, who was heard by witnesses to shout, 'This is for London Bridge.' Immediately after carrying out the attack, Osborne was surrounded by a hostile crowd, but he was saved from serious harm by the intervention of a local imam, Mohammed Mahmoud, who was able to persuade those present to leave it to the police and the courts to ensure that justice was served.

Following his conviction at Crown Court, Osborne was sentenced to more than forty years in jail. The trial judge observed that he had been 'rapidly radicalised over the internet, encountering and consuming material put out... from those determined to spread hatred of Muslims on the basis of their religion'. It was discovered that he had been reading material from the former EDL leader Tommy Robinson and the far right group Britain First. The judge continued: 'Over the course of a month or so, your mindset became one of malevolent hatred.'

But where on earth does that kind of deadly hatred come from?

Allport's Scale of Prejudice,[34] first developed by the psychologist Gordon Allport in the 1950s, offers some potential clues concerning the origins of hatred in its most extreme forms. His original scale ranked five escalating stages of prejudice, each more harmful than the one before:

Stage 1: Antilocution
The word antilocution means, quite literally, 'speaking against'. Allport starts out with the power of words, with the use of language as an expression of hate. Far from being harmless, words can start wars. The book of James in the New Testament goes so far as to suggest that 'the

tongue is a flame of fire. It is a whole world of wicked-ness ... it can set your whole life on fire.'[35] And the line between violent words and violent deeds can be a mighty thin one.

Stage 2: Avoidance

Avoidance marks the first point at which words alone come to an end and behaviour begins. Members of a particular group – defined according to race, belief, culture, gender, sexuality or any one of a thousand other things – become isolated and defined as the 'other'. They are regarded by those who stand apart from them with a combination of suspicion and fear. In many instances, they are held responsible for the ills of the world.

Stage 3: Discrimination

A group of people is discriminated against when they are denied basic rights or equal access to opportunities, goods and services. 'No Irish, no blacks, no dogs', as the old signs once said.

Stage 4: Physical Attack

This is the stage at which violence begins, either towards people or towards their property. These days we give it a name: hate crime. One of my old bosses, John Grieve – a former head of the Anti-Terrorist Branch – describes hate crime as 'the foothills of terrorism'.

Stage 5: Extermination
The final stage. Hitler called it 'the Final Solution'. This is the point on the scale at which a group that has already been isolated, discriminated against and attacked is placed in danger of complete extermination.

Dramatic though the progression and escalation of the scale may appear, history has demonstrated its truth. And according to Allport, what ends in genocide begins with words.

*

We appear to be living in a world characterised increasingly by fury, in which we yell ever more loudly at one another while the distance between us only grows. Old fault lines have broken wide open, between those who believe one thing and those who oppose them. Between us and them.

In Parliament, the Speaker of the House of Commons calls repeatedly for 'order', but there is none as the level of political debate descends once more into acrimony, with braying and bawling taking the place of any semblance of reasoned and rational conversation. And this from the people who are supposed to be in charge. Empowered in part by their example, public interaction disintegrates into animosity; fear and ferocity are written on the faces of ordinary people racing to be right or to exact revenge.

The media play their part with screaming headlines and sensationalist copy, battling for readers and vying for viewers in the age of twenty-four-hour news. One-eyed world views collide with commercial opportunity and the bottom line remains the bottom line: whatever sells and damn the consequences. All the while, the government minister won't listen to the journalist's questions and the journalist won't listen to the minister's answers. Each has their own point to make, their own blow to land, while the rest of us are left to hurl our exasperation at the TV.

The mainstream press shouting match is renewed and intensified on social media, where respectful conversation is abandoned swiftly in favour of hostile confrontation and cases are decided in the five-second court of online opinion. Emboldened by anonymity and abandoning conscience, voices clamour to blame and accuse. Everywhere you look is the rush to oppose, to hoist heads on spikes, to terrify opponents and strangers alike. The right to freedom of speech is exploited to justify freedom from responsibility for the consequences of anything we might choose to say. These are dangerous times.

Jo Cox was forty-one years old when she was murdered – shot and stabbed and left for dead in the street. She was a woman of remarkable character and courage who, prior to becoming the Member of Parliament for Batley and Spen in the north of England, had worked for Oxfam in roles that had exposed her to the realities of life in some of the most challenging places on earth. On entering Parliament following the 2015 general election, she gave her voice to the Syrian cause – to the urgent need to find solutions to the ongoing conflict, to the desperate requirement for humanitarian aid in the region and to the shattering experiences of innocent refugees attempting to flee. She decried the lack of a 'moral compass' in British government policy and was later described by *Economist* magazine as 'idealistic, diligent, likeable' and 'a living rebuttal' to the pervasive cynicism about politics and politicians in the UK.

She left behind her husband, Brendan, and their two young children.

Her killer was a fifty-two-year-old man named Thomas Mair: a white supremacist, a Nazi sympathiser, a furious far-right terrorist driven to murder. Jo Cox represented everything he hated. She had opened her ears and arms and heart to the outsiders that Mair – and too many others like him – believed were to blame for the ills of his small world. With a gun and a knife, in the middle of an otherwise nondescript day, he stole her from her family and her community. Given her early achievements and her evident potential as an MP, you might actually say that he stole her from us all.

Mair was detained about a mile from the scene by two unarmed police officers – PCs Craig Nicholls and Jonathan Wright – who, knowing that Jo had been shot and stabbed, tackled him to the ground and disarmed him. They recovered a gun, a knife and a bag of bullets. For their remarkable courage, they were later awarded the Queen's Gallantry Medal. And they were not the only brave men that day. Bernard Carter-Kenny was stabbed in the chest as he came to Jo's aid. He was seventy-seven years old, a member of the public who just happened to be passing by at the time of the attack, a man who risked his own life in an attempt to save Jo's. He was later awarded the George Medal, presented posthumously to his widow following his death from cancer.

During Mair's trial at the Old Bailey, the court heard that while attacking Jo, he had shouted, 'This is for Britain' and 'Britain First'. It is on such twisted logic that death is dealt. Police searches of his home following his arrest had recovered Nazi memorabilia and extremist literature. Searches of his internet browsing history had revealed more of the same.

In sentencing Mair to life imprisonment, the judge, Mr Justice Wilkie, described Jo as 'passionate, open-hearted, inclusive and generous'. Everything her murderer was not. Outside the court, following the hearing, Brendan Cox spoke about his late wife:

> 'To the world, Jo was a Member of Parliament, a campaigner, an activist and many other things. But first and foremost, she was a sister, a daughter, an auntie, a wife, and above all a mum to two young children who love her with all their being.'

Of Thomas Mair, the widower had only this to say:

> 'We feel nothing but pity for him; that his life was so devoid of love that his only way of finding meaning was to attack a defenceless woman who represented the best of our country in an act of supreme cowardice.'

Jo was murdered during a period of deeply polarised national debate about Britain's relationship with Europe, in the lead-up to the EU referendum. Reckless agitators were playing on the anxieties of ordinary people, not least about immigrants – those strangers from other places who stood accused of coming over here and stealing our jobs, exploiting our services, raping our women and abusing our children. The national atmosphere was fearful and febrile, as newspapers wrote toxic stories and politicians practised half-truths and deceptions. All the while they failed to acknowledge and articulate the overwhelmingly positive contributions of hundreds of thousands of immigrants – doctors and nurses and engineers and teachers and carers and all the rest – who have enhanced and enriched our country in more ways than we could count.

Somewhere in the midst of it all, a remarkable human being lost her life. Jo Cox's story is one of conscience; of public service and personal sacrifice; of words and their power; of rage unchallenged and unchecked; of a man of violence possessing weapons and cause. But it is also a story of humanity and hope. Jo was a champion of outsiders, a voice of calm and reason and kindness and experience, who had once pointed out the simple fact that 'we have more in common than that which divides us'. Dr King had it right all along: hatred cannot drive out hatred; only love can do that.

X. *A Question of Belief*

Five teenage boys and one teenage girl. They were children really. It was 2009 and I was working as the superintendent in charge of uniformed operations for the borough of Islington in north London. I was briefed about the case the morning after it all happened.

The boys had prepared everything in advance: it was the very definition of premeditated, a crime so wicked that it leaves me struggling to comprehend it even now. The five of them had somehow got hold of the keys to a flat that was empty during the day. And that was where they took her. I can't recall now whether it was deception or fear that got her through the front door, but apparently, no passer-by saw or heard anything that caused them enough concern to call the police. The girl knew the boys; at some level perhaps she even trusted them.

They took her into a bedroom, and there they raped her, one at a time, while the others looked on. Once they'd finished with her, they just threw her out into the street while they attempted to remove every evidential trace that they had ever been there. They reckoned without her courage, though. She told her story to the police, and her attackers were tracked down and forced to face the consequences of their crimes.

Horrifying though that story is, my fear is that we risk becoming desensitised to what it tells us – that we are in danger of losing sight of what is happening in the real world. Women and girls get raped all the time, in both the fiction of films and the fact of sordid internet streams. Women and girls get raped in newspaper articles and in the third item on the local evening news. It all becomes far too familiar and the full weight of it starts to lose meaning and significance for those of us who are just passing by. Perhaps we would simply prefer not to know.

But the fact is that I do know. Every police officer knows, because we see it and hear it and face the reality of it throughout our working lives. And I will never forget the story of that young Islington girl – of the agony and terror and trauma she suffered that day.

*

In 2013, the Home Office, the Ministry of Justice and the Office for National Statistics published a joint report providing an overview of patterns of sexual offending in England and Wales.[36] The report's authors estimated (using three years' worth of data from the Crime Survey for England and Wales: 2009/10–2011/12) that every year, 78,000 women aged between sixteen and fifty-nine are victims of rape, attempted rape or sexual assault by penetration. That is an astonishing number – 78,000 women and girls – but it's also a significant underestimate. It doesn't include anyone under the age of sixteen, or over the age of fifty-nine. It doesn't include anyone living in non-residential household settings; for example, the homeless, or students in college halls of residence. It doesn't include anyone in Scotland or Northern Ireland. And it is just for three specific categories of offending, leaving a whole host of other horrors unaccounted for. Then there is the basic fact that sexual offences of all kinds remain among the most under-reported of all crimes. In her independent review into how rape complaints are handled by public authorities in England and Wales, Baroness Vivien Stern estimated that just 11 per cent of rape victims report their crime to the police.[37]

It is important to acknowledge here that, of course, men can suffer sexual assault too. The 2017 Crime Survey[38] estimated that 8,000 men aged sixteen to fifty-nine had been victims of rape, attempted rape or assault by penetration in the preceding twelve months. It matters that we acknowledge the reality of male rape for the same reasons that it matters we acknowledge the reality of male victims of domestic violence. But, as with DV, I want to focus here on female victimisation – not because male victims matter less or because their trauma is somehow less real or deserving of attention; it is simply a question of scale.

The history of the police response to serious sexual assault allegations is chequered at best. That is in part because sexual offences can be immensely complex and challenging to investigate. But it is also because policing has, on occasions

– both individually and institutionally – got things terribly wrong.

In October 2012, a former Met detective constable was sentenced to sixteen months in prison after admitting thirteen counts of misconduct in a public office. His crimes included the failure to properly investigate a number of rape and sexual offences allegations and the falsification of entries on police databases. The DC, who had been sacked by the Met in April 2011, was based in a south-east London Sapphire unit – one of a number of specialist sexual offences teams set up to professionalise the police response to these horrendous crimes. The people he failed included a ninety-six-year-old woman believed to have been a victim of rape and a forty-nine-year-old care home resident suffering with severe brain damage who alleged that she had been raped by a member of the home's staff. The former officer admitted his guilt and suggested that he had no one to blame but himself.

On occasions, though, the basis of concern has been much broader than the actions (or inactions) of a lone individual. In early 2013, the Independent Police Complaints Commission (IPCC) published a report titled 'Southwark Sapphire Unit's local practices for the reporting and investigation of sexual offences, July 2008–September 2009'. It was the fifth IPCC investigation into Southwark borough and the ninth overall concerning the Met's response to allegations of sexual violence. It makes for deeply uncomfortable reading.

The following extract is taken from the IPCC commissioner's foreword:

The review found that Southwark Sapphire unit was underperforming and overstretched and officers of all ranks, often unfamiliar with sexual offence work, felt under pressure to improve performance and meet targets. Its sanction-detection rate (the proportion of recorded crimes that proceed to prosecution) was poor, and management focused on hitting this target as a measure of success.

We found that Southwark Sapphire had implemented its own standard operating procedure over this period to meet these targets. Essentially, this took the form of encouraging... victims to retract allegations (so that no crime was recorded) in cases where it was thought that they might later withdraw or not reach the standard for prosecution (which would have been recorded as an unsolved crime). This resulted in the close questioning of victims before they even met an officer trained in dealing with sex crimes and the widespread use of retraction statements – including in cases where this was clearly inappropriate. This local standard operating procedure, authorised by senior officers, increased the number of incidents that were classified as 'no crime' and therefore increased the sanction-detection rates for the unit.

The approach of failing to believe victims in the first instance was wholly inappropriate and went against the first principle of the MPS standard operating procedure:

to believe the victim until evidence demonstrated otherwise. This pressure to meet targets as a measure of success, rather than focusing on the outcome for the victim, resulted in the police losing sight of what policing is about.

This was not simply a case of hitting the target and missing the point. It was a case of police officers failing utterly to hold true to the very reasons why they were there in the first place – reasons that had once been articulated to me with beautiful simplicity by a group of primary school children: to help good people and to catch bad people. Yes, the Southwark Sapphire unit was overstretched and under pressure. Yes, some of its staff lacked experience. But those things cannot be offered as excuses. I'm not even sure they can be presented as mitigation. The officers concerned, particularly those in charge, failed in their most basic duty: they failed to protect the public.

If there is any consolation to be found in this sorry tale, it is that the Met – and policing more widely – has since made enormous improvements to the ways in which sexual offences are investigated, not least in placing a far greater emphasis on the level of support and care offered to victims. But there is still much to be done. There are many reasons why the victims of rape and sexual assault might be reluctant to report those crimes to the authorities. A basic mistrust of the police is very high on that list, no doubt aggravated by the kinds of failings identified in the 2013 IPCC report, but there are other reasons too.

Some victims are reluctant to subject themselves to the intrusive medical procedures that are a vital element of the initial police response to any allegation of rape. Cases may stand or fall on forensic evidence that can only be obtained by means of intimate medical examination, and, already traumatised by the crime itself, the prospect of any further physical ordeal might understandably be too much to bear. Other victims are anxious to avoid becoming involved in a long-drawn-out criminal investigation, the outcome of which is far from certain. The fact is that only a tiny proportion of rapes reported to the police result in an eventual conviction at court: figures published by the Victim's Commissioner in August 2019 suggest that just one in every fifty rape cases results in a conviction.[39] Some victims are terrified by the prospect that they will be forced to face their abuser during a trial. The idea of being asked to sit in the same courtroom as the person who raped them, while being subjected to hostile cross-examination by a defence barrister intent on dissecting every last detail of their sex lives, is more than enough to distress even the bravest. For many, though, the fear takes hold long before the question of formal criminal proceedings becomes a possibility. It begins even before the first call to the police is made. And it is expressed in the form of a simple question: 'Is anyone going to believe me?'

It is this basic notion of belief that lies at the very heart of the police response to allegations of sexual violence.

*

At some point in my professional life, I learned the policing ABC:

Accept nothing.
Believe no one.
Challenge everything.

My old detective superintendent had it pinned on the wall next to his desk as a kind of mission statement, an exhortation to every investigator who happened to pass by. If I'm honest, I never much liked it. It seemed to me to characterise the kind of stereotypical hard-bitten cynicism that belonged to another policing age. But I understood where the sentiments came from and why they still had such resonance.

Operational police officers are lied to practically every day of their working lives. It is as inevitable as it is depressing. They deal with people proven time and again to be unfamiliar with anything remotely resembling the truth, people who will say whatever it takes to get away with whatever it is they might have done. Some criminals are hopeless at lying, ready to say the first thing that comes into their heads, only for their story to unravel in the face of even the most basic inquiries. But others have spent a lifetime mastering the dark arts of deceit and they are very good at it. When they aren't confining themselves to bland 'no comment' answers in response to every question put, they are perfectly willing to tell you almost anything, so long as none of it is the actual truth. It takes immense investigative patience and skill to find them out.

Within a few months of starting out as a PC, I had lost count of the number of people who had tried to mislead me. If I had accepted everything, believed all of them and challenged nothing, I would likely have struggled to solve a single crime or convict a single criminal. Somehow, I had to develop a healthy degree of scepticism without becoming cynical – to nurture a persistently enquiring mind without becoming world-weary. And that wasn't the only point of concern. One minute I might have been dealing with a bare-faced lying suspect, but the next I could have been speaking to the victim of a rape, and the danger was that I applied the policing ABC equally to both of them. Over time, my starting point became one of practised disbelief – the product of professional experience, compounded over time. Suspects almost always lied to me, but sometimes victims did as well. And what of the consequences on those comparatively rare occasions when that happened? If I believed a lying suspect, then a guilty man might go free. If I believed a lying victim, then an innocent man might go to jail. And which of those two things is worse?

In the last twenty years, a frequently repeated criticism of the police response to rape has been that investigating officers have too often appeared to be (and in many cases have indeed been) disbelieving of the accounts given by those who claim to have been victims. In such cases, the approach taken by officers is directly contrary to established police policy – alluded to in the IPCC report quoted earlier and clearly set out in guidance issued to Met investigators as far back as 2002: 'It is the policy of the MPS to accept allegations made by the victim in the first instance as being truthful. An allegation will only be considered as falling short of a substantiated allegation after a full and thorough investigation.'

But the evident tension between victim belief and disbelief has been painfully slow to resolve. In the foreword to her 2010 report into how rape complaints are handled, Baroness Stern offered this reflection on her more than forty years of involvement in crime-related work: 'I have often voiced concern that we have failed to understand what a caring society should be doing to respond to those who have been harmed by crime.' She continued: 'John Worboys and Kirk Reid [both notorious serial rapists] were men who managed to rape and assault many women before they were stopped, because the police in London did not take the victims seriously enough when they came to report what had happened to them and rape was not a sufficiently high priority for some of the police at the time.'

The Stern Review is quick to acknowledge the positives evident in rape investigation at the time the report was compiled – not least 'a wide range of deeply dedicated men and women whose work has helped to bring a traumatised person through a most terrible experience' – but the basic concerns expressed are abundantly clear. And they remained stubbornly apparent in the years that followed.

In November 2014, the *Guardian* published a blog titled 'How the police are letting sexual assault victims down'.[40] The article highlighted the fact that only about 15 per cent of those who experience sexual violence report it to the police. The piece was written in the same month that Her Majesty's Inspectorate of Constabulary published an official report suggesting that 26 per cent of all sexual offences reported to the police (including rape) were not recorded as crimes.[41]

HMIC also suggested that one in five of all police decisions to 'no crime' existing rape reports was incorrect. Speaking at the time – specifically about this issue of crime recording – Sir Tom Winsor, the civilian head of the Inspectorate, declared in an interview with the BBC: 'The police need to institutionalise a culture of believing the victim. Every time.'[42]

His views echoed the broader concerns that had been repeated by critics for years and that were being picked up with increasing insistence by the mainstream news media. It was clear that the old policing ABC was out of step with the times, certainly so far as sexual offences investigations were concerned, and that an alternative approach was being demanded – one based on the principle of victim belief. Policing was being provided with an unequivocal set of directions, but rarely is anything in life – and especially in policing – straightforward.

In late 2014, a man identified by the pseudonym 'Nick' came forward and made a series of stunning criminal allegations that included the suggestion of a VIP paedophile ring operating in and around Westminster. All sorts of high-profile names were mentioned and all hell seemed to break loose, not least in Parliament and the press. The notorious cases of Jimmy Savile and others, in which public figures had been allowed to get away with a significant number of heinous crimes, were still fresh in the memory, and there was a relentless and very public clamour for the facts of this new case to be made known.

Evidently, the starting position for the police investigation team was to believe Nick. And I have absolutely no doubt that the pendulum swing from 'believe no one' to 'believe the victim, every time' was at the forefront of their minds. One of the senior officers leading the investigation even went so far as to describe the allegations as 'credible and true'.

Except that they were neither. Nick had made it all up.

With remarkable speed, some of the same people – particularly in the media – who had been deriding the police for failing to believe alleged victims of serious sexual assault began to hammer them for believing an alleged victim of serious sexual assault. In February 2018, the *Guardian* ran a headline asking: 'After the lessons of the 1990s satanic abuse scandal, why was "Nick" believed?'[43] There appeared to be no hint of self-awareness or irony in the query. Sometimes, police officers feel damned if they do, and damned if they don't.

My instinct and my preference is to trust the word of a victim over the word of a suspect every single time. And in the vast majority of cases, that would likely prove to be the right thing to do. But my effectiveness as a police officer was never founded on the notion of blind belief; rather on the dispassionate requirement to follow the evidence, wherever it might take me. Because in the search for real and lasting justice, only the truth will do.

Beyond the debate about belief, there is a second question that contributes to the uniquely complex intractability of so many rape investigations. It is the question of consent. In almost every case, it is one person's word against another.

In the rape investigation involving the two alcoholics that I mentioned in chapter I, the question of consent was the only one that exercised us. Both parties agreed that sex had taken place. They even agreed on the finer details of what had gone on between them. The only point of dispute was whether she had been a willing participant. She said no, he said yes, and it was left to us to work out whether there was any prospect of getting anywhere close to the truth of it all. It's a struggle faced by rape investigators time and time again.

Many years ago, I sat down in my west London office in the company of a young sergeant who had no idea why I'd asked to see him. Half an hour earlier, I'd been reading through the statement of a reported rape victim. The sergeant had been off duty when he met her at a nightclub and it appeared that there might have been some sort of spark between them. He ended up as one of a small group she invited back to her house later that night, but at no point did she suggest that she might want to have sex with him. When he climbed into her bed later on, she was clear in her view that it was both uninvited and unwelcome. As was everything else that followed.

I looked at him and it was evident he had no idea that he was about to be arrested by two of his colleagues who were waiting in the office next door. I asked him if he remembered the night in question. He said that he did. I asked him if he remembered the girl. He said he did. When I told him that she had accused him of rape, his face flickered and turned grey and folded in front of me. Frightened and disbelieving, he sat there in his police uniform, with his career and life and future in the balance, all to be determined by the answer given to the question of consent.

I'm unaware of the outcome of that particular case, but the

circumstances involved are typical of so many others. When it comes to sex, consent is surely the most important consideration of all. Because no must always mean no. And there really are no exceptions, no defences or any mitigating factors.

The amount that a woman has had to drink is entirely irrelevant. In fact, in my view, the presence of alcohol simply makes the crime worse. It is only predators who take advantage of intoxication. A slurred 'no' means exactly the same as a sober 'no'. And in circumstances where a woman has drunk so much that she is no longer able to give any kind of informed response, there should never even be a question for her to answer.

The way in which a woman is dressed has got absolutely nothing to do with it either. I don't care how short the skirt or how high the heels. The extent to which a woman is willing to engage in any kind of foreplay is irrelevant too. It remains her absolute right to say 'no' or 'no more' at any point along the way, and it remains his absolute responsibility to pay heed. She is never 'asking for it'.

The fact that a woman is a man's wife or girlfriend has got nothing to do with it either. Something like 90 per cent of all victims of rape know their attacker. A woman is not some kind of possession, to be used and abused and cast aside. Her body is her own; her choices are hers alone. And consent matters every single time.

*

As a dad to daughters, I find myself increasingly concerned by the highly sexualised nature of the world that my girls are growing up in. I'm troubled deeply by all the ways in which women are objectified and womanhood is defined by body shape and perceived sex appeal and an entirely misplaced set of ideas about skin-deep beauty. It's there on the sides of buses and in endless social media feeds. It's there on the pages of glossy magazines and in every other part of the media. It's there in porn.

During my 1980s adolescence, most porn remained out of my reach – on the top shelf of the newsagents or in the small X-rated section of the local video store. But the 1990s saw the beginnings of online porn and the advent of pay-per-view downloading. Initially, the requirement to use a credit card to access films and pictures acted as an informal age verification mechanism – protecting some children at least from seeing the sorts of things that no child should ever see – but all of that changed when access to porn became free at the point of consumption. Anyone could watch, children included.

Whatever your views on the rights and wrongs of porn per se, what cannot be in any doubt is the devastating impact its easy availability is having on the lives of children, who are growing up in a porn-soaked world. As a police officer, the ubiquity was always the thing that troubled me the most. Kids with any kind of internet connection now get their sex education online, and you don't need to be a puritan dinosaur to share an enormous sense of concern about the consequences of that.

What is it that boys now expect? And what is it that girls are placed under endless pressure to accept? What is it that passes for healthy and normal when it comes to sex? The Islington gang rape happened in the early years of online porn streaming, and I believe there is a connection between those two things. Of course rape happened before the internet – I don't think that porn is exclusively to blame for the rise in sexual offending – but there seems no end to the further damage done by the so-called advance of technology. It's not unlike the situation I've observed with boys who carry knives. Sex offenders are getting younger; much younger. In America, there are children as young as six on the sex offenders register. And at the same time, the seriousness of the crimes being committed appears to be escalating. Porn is fantasy; the people portrayed in it are not real. And it is precisely this dehumanisation that can lead a fourteen-year-old boy with no available alternative in terms of healthy sex education or role modelling to imagine that he can have whatever he wants, whenever and wherever he wants it. We are now faced with the compelling need for far greater restrictions on the availability of pornography, beginning with the implementation of a mandatory block on access to online porn for anyone under the age of eighteen.

*

In March 2014, the Centre for Social Justice (CSJ) and the London-based youth charity XLP published a brief joint report concerning the involvement of girls in gangs.[44] In it, you can read the story of 'Girl X'.

At the age of twelve, she had sex with a fourteen-year-old gang member, unaware of the fact that he was filming the whole thing. He later threatened to send the footage to her family and to post it online unless she agreed to have sex with any other member of the gang who wanted it. Terrified, she agreed. Terrified, she was raped every single week. Terrified, she introduced other girls to the gang in the hope that they might then leave her alone. And so it went on, from one girl to the next.

The CSJ/XLP report also makes reference to a 2008 article in the *Guardian*, published under the headline 'Blood Sisters'.[45] In it, a former gang member called Amy described the reality that she and her peers faced: 'The boys would treat us as their bitches, phone whoever they felt like fucking, order them to come over, and most girls would drop everything and do whatever was wanted.'

NSPCC figures from 2009 suggest that one in three teenage girls who had been in a relationship had experienced sexual violence from a partner.[46] A 2010 YouGov poll indicated that almost one in three teenage girls had experienced groping or some other form of unwelcome sexual touching at school – one of the few places where they might reasonably expect to be safe.[47] In 2013, the Office of the Children's Commissioner suggested that the exposure of young people to pornography was linked directly to unrealistic attitudes about sex and to beliefs that women were sex objects.[48]

In 2017, the charity Barnardo's published figures suggesting that, in the space of just four years – aggravated, undoubtedly, by rapid advances in technology and the advent of new phenomena such as 'sexting' – the number of allegations involving children committing sexual offences against other children had risen by a staggering 78 per cent.[49] And those were just the cases that had been reported to police. The culture of 'no snitching' that so often persists among groups of young people means that the true scale of the problem remains hidden from us all.

And it's not just the stories of young victims that are troubling; it is the tales told by adults too. In late 2011, I was responsible for leading Operation Ursus, a joint initiative involving the Met, British Transport Police, Thames Valley Police and the Borders Agency. The intention was to target the widespread criminal activities of organised gangs from Eastern Europe. I was borough commander for Camden at the time, and my local area was being plagued by pickpockets and suspects stealing laptops and handbags. The problem was not one of violence – no one was being physically harmed during the commission of the thefts – it was one of scale: the perpetrators were getting away with tens of thousands of pounds of stolen property. The same was happening in the boroughs surrounding us and throughout the London Transport network.

The operation ran for several weeks, but part way through, we planned two days of concentrated action that involved the execution of multiple search warrants at addresses right across London. Early on the first morning, I joined one of the teams raiding a terraced house in east London, not far from the Olympic Park. We were expecting to find large quantities of stolen property. There were a couple of Eastern European girls in the house, who initially weren't saying very much. I went into one of the upstairs bedrooms with the intention of looking for stolen credit cards and mobile phones. It was sparsely furnished – just a double bed and a small chest of drawers – and surprisingly clean. I opened the top drawer and discovered that it was full of condoms. The house wasn't being used to store stolen property; it was being used as a brothel. The same criminal gangs that were relieving tourists of their computers and cameras were trafficking girls into the country for the purposes of prostitution.

The legal slave trade might have been abolished for the best part of two hundred years, but there are now more slaves in the world than at any previous point in human history. As with any hidden crime, it is difficult to estimate the true numbers, but according to the International Labour Organisation, there are currently more than forty million victims of human trafficking worldwide.[50] Seventy-one per cent of them are women and girls; twenty-five per cent of them are children. They have been enslaved for a variety of reasons, including labour exploitation and domestic servitude, with almost five million of them being forced into the sex trade. They are working in brothels and strip clubs, on webcams and porn sets, on sex lines and in chat rooms, in escort agencies and massage parlours.

It is one thing to make a conscious and informed choice to sell your body for sex. It is another thing entirely to be stolen from your homeland and forced to do so. And once again, we look to the police – and to their partners in the National Crime Agency and Borders Agency – to catch the traffickers and to rescue those trafficked. Except that, as with every other serious crime problem facing us as a society, we are never, ever going to be able to arrest our way out of it.

In December 2018, the anti-slavery charity Stop the Traffik published a blog titled 'Why arresting people won't stop human trafficking.[51] It was written by Neil Giles, a former police officer who had been appointed to a senior role at the charity. Neil explained that while every arrest of a trafficker was undoubtedly a good thing, it was only a drop in the ocean of modern slavery. He wrote: 'The problem of human trafficking is all too large and amorphous for arrest and prosecution to stop it.'

He pointed out that the trade is worth somewhere in the region of £150 billion a year. It is 'a global, agile enterprise driven by easy profit and low risks'. Given that enforcement alone will only ever have a limited effect, Stop the Traffik suggest three alternative responses to the problem. The first is intelligence-led prevention – the disruption of criminal networks at source. Rather than attempting to rescue slaves after they have been transported into the UK, it is undoubtedly much better to protect and safeguard them in their home country; to frustrate every attempt to take them in the first place. The second response is to 'build resilience' in those same countries of origin, connecting, resourcing and training networks of individuals and organisations committed to the anti-slavery cause. The third response is to tell the stories of those who have been enslaved – to educate the rest of us about the reality and scale of the problem, to teach us how to spot the signs of modern slavery and how to respond when we do.

As with every other problem set out in this book, we need to understand that the challenges of human trafficking – and of sexual offending more generally – will never be solved by policing and law enforcement alone. They are concerns for the whole of society that demand a response from us all.

XI. *On the Register*

I can still see the face of Victoria Climbié, pictured in the newspapers wide-eyed and smiling: a beautiful little girl wearing a tartan dress and red woollen cardigan. She was just eight years old when she was murdered by the very people who were supposed to protect her. My involvement in her case was minimal, but her story remains etched in my memory.

Victoria was born in the Ivory Coast in November 1991. Seven years later, she left home in the care of her great-aunt, Marie-Thérèse Kouao, for the promise of an education and a better life overseas. Having travelled first to France, the two of them arrived in London in April 1999. There, Kouao met a man named Carl Manning and they started a relationship.

Victoria died at their hands less than a year later, the victim of abuse as wicked and depraved as anything I have ever come across.

In early 2001, her two killers were sentenced to life in

prison. In January 2003, the Laming Inquiry into the circumstances of Victoria's death was published.[52] And it reads like
a horror story:

> Victoria spent much of her last days, in the winter of
> 1999–2000, living and sleeping in a bath in an unheated
> bathroom, bound hand and foot inside a bin bag, lying
> in her own urine and faeces. It is not surprising then that
> towards the end of her short life, Victoria was stooped like
> an old lady and could walk only with great difficulty.
>
> When Victoria was admitted to the North Middlesex
> Hospital on the evening of 24 February 2000, she
> was desperately ill. She was bruised, deformed and
> malnourished. Her temperature was so low it could not
> be recorded on the hospital's standard thermometer. Dr
> Lesley Alsford, the consultant responsible for Victoria's
> care on that occasion, said, 'I had never seen a case like it
> before. It is the worst case of child abuse and neglect that I
> have ever seen.'[53]

Victoria died a day later. She had endured horrendous
beatings at the hands of Kouao and Manning. She had been
hit with a shoe, a coat hanger, a hammer and a bicycle chain.
Traces of her blood were found on Manning's football boots.
Dr Nat Carey, the Home Office pathologist who conducted
the post-mortem examination, recorded 128 separate injuries
to her body. Her heart, lungs and kidneys had all failed. In
his evidence to the inquiry, Dr Carey said: 'All non-accidental
injuries to children are awful and difficult for everybody to

deal with, but in terms of the nature and extent of the injury, and the almost systematic nature of the inflicted injury, I certainly regard this as the worst I have ever dealt with, and it is just about the worst I have ever heard of.'

I find it difficult and painful to read, never mind record, these things. But the truth of it is that it's too important not to, not least because Victoria's death would appear to have been entirely preventable. Lord Laming's report points out that prior to her death, Victoria had been known to three separate housing authorities, four Social Services departments, two Met Police child protection teams (CPTs), a specialist centre managed by the NSPCC, and the two hospitals she was admitted to because of suspected deliberate harm. She had only been in Britain for eleven months when she died, but in that short space of time she had been failed by at least four separate statutory agencies. I can't help feeling that in some sense, she was failed by us all. There were twelve separate occasions on which those in positions of authority might have intervened to save her life, but each time the opportunity was missed.

I agree with Lord Laming's assessment that 'the suffering and death of Victoria was a gross failure of the system and was inexcusable', though we must never lose sight of the fact that it was Kouao and Manning alone who were responsible for murdering her.

My fleeting connection with Victoria's story came in the autumn of 2000, nine months after her death. I was working for the Racial and Violent Crime Task Force at the time and was asked to meet with the commander in charge of

Operation Bluemartin, the Met's high-level response to Victoria's murder and to the identified police failings that had preceded it. My senior colleagues were, quite rightly, treating the case as a critical incident, and given RAVCTF's experience in dealing with and advising on a number of other high-profile murder investigations, the commander was concerned to ensure that she had thought through every possible aspect of her responsibilities. In addition to talking through the circumstances of the murder and the forthcoming trial of Kouao and Manning, we discussed a range of broader issues, including the resourcing of the Met's child protection teams, the nature of the relationships between the teams and their statutory partners in Health and Social Services, and the ongoing discipline investigations being carried out into the conduct of ten police officers who had been involved in Victoria's case. We spoke about the importance of providing appropriate support to members of Victoria's biological family, and about the need to seek out the critical friendship of independent advisers who would test and challenge the Met's thinking and decision-making at every point along the way. But while there might have been some marginal sense of satisfaction to be gained from trying to put things right, it was all far too late for one little girl.

In many respects, the murder of Victoria Climbié represented a watershed moment in the care and protection of children in the UK. The Laming Inquiry had been one of the largest of its kind that this country has ever seen, with hearings that lasted for ten months and evidence taken from 150 witnesses. It led directly to the publication of the *Every*

Child Matters government green paper and was the catalyst for the Children Act 2004. But no matter how much might have changed and what any of us might have learned in the years immediately following Victoria's death, the truth is that there would be others like her.

*

In 2018, the National Society for the Prevention of Cruelty to Children published a report titled 'How safe are our children?'[54] It offered a series of harrowing indicators concerning the safety and well-being of children in this country:

- Child homicide: in 2016/17, there were 98 child homicides in the UK: 91 in England, 3 in Wales and 4 in Scotland.
- Child suicide: the suicide rate among young people in England and Wales had started to rise. In 2016, 198 teenagers aged 15–19 took their own lives.
- Cruelty and neglect: in England alone in 2016/17, there were 13,591 reported instances of child cruelty and neglect. The figures had risen when compared with the previous year in England, Wales and Northern Ireland. The only exception was Scotland. But in every single part of the UK, there appeared to be a long-term upward trend in the number of children on the Child Protection Register and on child protection plans. Neglect appeared to be the primary driver. In fact, in both England and Northern Ireland, the number of children who were being 'looked after' by the state as a consequence of neglect or abuse was the highest on record.

- Violence: in 2016/17, there were 212,000 recorded child (aged 10–15) victims of violence.
- Sexual offences: there had been a steady increase in the number of sexual offences committed against children in all UK nations. It was suggested that some of this change was likely attributable to improvements in crime recording practices and perhaps even to greater levels of confidence in the police, but neither of those things should be allowed to distract from the stark truth that thousands of children are being sexually assaulted in this country. In England in 2016/17 alone, more than 6,400 children under the age of 13 and more than 6,600 children between the ages of 13 and 16 reported having been raped. Both figures represented an increase on the previous twelve months: more than 13,000 children under the age of 16 raped in a single year. And, as ever, the understandable reluctance of many sexual assault victims to come forward means that the official numbers will always be a significant underestimate.
- Calls to Childline: in 2016/17, there were 66,218 calls to the NSPCC crisis phone number. 66,218 cries for help.

There were children crying for help in the town of Rother-ham for many years before anyone in a position of power or authority started to pay attention. More than 1,400 children by one credible estimate.[55]

In October 2018, a group of seven men were convicted of a linked series of serious sexual offences committed against five girls over a seven-year period. The suspects had used alcohol, drugs and threats of violence to control the girls. Then they had assaulted and, in the case of six of the suspects, raped them. It was the latest prosecution to emerge from the work of Operation Stovewood, an investigation led by the National Crime Agency (NCA) into child sexual exploitation (CSE) in and around Rotherham between 1997 and 2013.

Evidence of systematic abuse of children in the area had been noted as far back as the 1990s, but nothing substantive had been done about it. It wasn't until 2010 that the first group of suspects was prosecuted. Five British Pakistani men were convicted of offences committed against girls aged twelve to sixteen. In 2012, eight British Pakistani men and one Afghan asylum-seeker were convicted of trafficking and a number of serious sexual offences, including rape. Their crimes dated back over the course of many years.

I mention the ethnicity of the suspects here only because it has been the source of so much debate and controversy as the Rotherham story has unfolded. There is a suggestion that one of the reasons for the inexcusable delays in bringing these men to justice was a fear on the part of some professionals that they would be accused of racism if they had been seen to pursue the suspects too vigorously when the allegations first came to light: racial sensitivity and community tension being apparent in divided neighbourhoods where the mere suggestion of racist behaviour, proven or otherwise, might prove to be career-ending. I understand the fear. But I also recognise the responsibility that every police officer has to follow the evidence, and to identify and pursue suspects on the basis of the crimes they have committed, irrespective of the colour of their skin.

In 2013, Professor Alexis Jay was asked by the local council to conduct an independent inquiry into the events of the preceding sixteen years. The Jay Report – which included the 'conservative' estimate of 1,400 abuse victims – was published in 2014: 'It is hard to describe the appalling nature of the abuse that child victims suffered. They were raped by multiple perpetrators, trafficked to other towns and cities in the north of England, abducted, beaten and intimidated. There were examples of children who had been doused in petrol and threatened with being set alight, threatened with guns, made to witness brutally violent rapes and threatened they would be next if they told anyone. Girls as young as eleven were raped by large numbers of male perpetrators.'[56]

As I read that last extract over and over again, I try to put myself in the place of just one of those girls, but I don't even know where to begin. To be eleven; to be raped; to be used up and discarded when there is nothing left of you to take.

The Jay Report is withering in its assessment of those who were supposed to be in charge at the time of the abuse. It suggests that 'the collective failures of political and officer leadership were blatant' and says that the police 'gave no operational priority to CSE'. That latter allegation certainly rings true to me. Policing during the 1990s and 2000s was governed by performance cultures and targets that did little or nothing to keep some of the most vulnerable in society safe. We had specialist departments dealing with sexual offences and child abuse, but as a uniformed officer overseeing general front-line policing operations during that time, I can barely recall senior officers ever mentioning CSE as a priority. In any case, we were far too busy chasing robbers and burglars.

As borough commander for Camden from 2010 to 2012, my performance (and that of all my officers and staff) was measured against a series of indicators that became known as 'the MOPAC 7' – seven specific crime types that the Mayor's Office for Policing and Crime had determined should be the focus of our efforts.

1. Burglary
2. Criminal damage
3. Theft from motor vehicles
4. Theft of motor vehicles
5. Violence with injury
6. Robbery
7. Theft from the person

Some of those things were undoubtedly important – certainly violence, robbery and burglary – but there was nothing in there about sexual offences and nothing about CSE, child abuse or human trafficking. There was no explicit mention of knife crime or domestic violence either. It was almost as if those things didn't matter. The fact is that I was far more likely to get a query from HQ about a series of mobile phone snatches than I was to get a call about a series of rapes.

When, in 2012, I started to pick up some local intelligence about the potential exploitation of young people living in a nearby children's home, there was nothing in my entire performance framework that compelled me to do a single thing about it. It's not something I was measured on or was ever likely to be asked questions about. And in any case, the kids who went missing from homes like the one in Camden always came back a day or two later and never told us what had happened to them while they were gone, so what was the point in taking details for yet another 'misper' report when it was likely to contain exactly the same limited information as the one we had filed just the week before? I had failed to fully appreciate what was happening to those children while they were missing; I had failed to acknowledge the strong probability that they were being exploited and trafficked and drugged and raped and otherwise abused in a thousand different ways.

When the Camden intelligence started to come through, it was only a whisper from my conscience that stopped me ignoring it completely. When I asked one of my DIs to take a closer look, I was acutely aware of the fact that he was facing any number of other performance pressures and that mine was an additional request he could doubtless have done without. I realise now that we should have pushed even harder than we did, but I was moved to a new posting shortly afterwards and I lost track of what happened to the children who were the subject of the original concern. This was in the days before the Jay Report – before the stories of a town in the north had been told in a city in the south.

The situation has improved in Rotherham in recent times, not least with the establishment by the council of a central team in children's social care to work alongside the police in safeguarding young lives. That said, any emerging sense of optimism is tempered immediately by the realisation, articulated in Professor Jay's report, that 'the team struggles to keep pace with the demands of its workload'. Between March 2015 and December 2018, the total number of children in care in Rotherham rose by more than 50 per cent, from 407 to 634.

And, of course, it was never just Rotherham. There have been further scandals exposed in places like Rochdale, Oxford and Bristol. An article published in the *Daily Telegraph* in March 2018 pointed to the town of Telford and allegations that as many as a thousand children may have been abused there, in cases dating as far back as the 1980s.[57] Professor Jay continued to lead a wide-ranging independent inquiry into child sexual abuse, gathering evidence from across the country. Between December 2016 and April 2018, five separate public hearings were held and at least a thousand victim and survivor stories were recorded. It ought to be noted that the scope of the inquiry stretches far beyond the archetypal run-down neighbourhoods of the inner city and into the Anglican and Roman Catholic churches and the fee-paying public schools of Downside and Ampleforth. The inquiry team published an interim report in 2018,[58] and in it they highlighted the absence of any kind of consistent, open societal conversation about the realities of CSE: 'Children will be better protected from sexual abuse if society is prepared to discuss the issue openly and frankly.'

We need to talk, and not just about sexual abuse, but about neglect and violence too. Children need to be both seen and heard.

Peter Connelly was born on 1 March 2006. He died on 3 August 2007, at the age of just seventeen months. You might remember him as 'Baby P', the pseudonym given to him while reporting restrictions remained in place during the trial of the people who killed him. During his short, agonising life, he sustained more than fifty separate physical injuries. The findings from his post-mortem examination included eight fractured ribs and a broken back. The timeline of Peter's brief life makes for almost unbearably bleak reading.

March 2006: Peter is born in London

June 2006: Peter's mother Tracey Connelly starts a relationship with Steven Barker

November 2006: Barker moves into the family home

December 2006: Connelly is arrested after a GP identifies bruises on Peter's face and chest

January 2007: after five weeks spent in the care of a family friend, Peter is returned home

February 2007: a former social worker writes to the Department of Health, raising concerns about the standard of child protection services in Haringey, Peter's home borough

April 2007: Peter is admitted to the North Middlesex Hospital; his injuries include two black eyes and swelling on the side of his head

May 2007: Peter is taken back to the same hospital after a social worker identifies marks on his face; medical staff identify several different areas of bruising and scratching; his mother is arrested again

June 2007: Barker's brother, Jason Owen, moves into the family home

July 2007: further injuries to Peter's face and hands are hidden from a social worker after they are covered with chocolate

2 August 2007: after her case has been reviewed by the Crown Prosecution Service, Connelly is told by police that she will not be prosecuted

3 August 2007: Baby Peter dies

November 2008: Connelly, Barker and Owen are convicted of causing Peter's death

November 2008: the government announces a formal inquiry into the circumstances of Peter's life and death

Unsurprisingly, Peter's story caused a public firestorm. The *Sun* ran a front page that carried the headline 'Blood on their Hands'. They set up a petition calling for the dismissal of senior figures in Haringey Council (the same local authority that had been criticised heavily following the murder of Victoria Climbié), publishing photographs of Sharon Shoesmith, the council's director of children's services, and Maria Ward, one of the social workers with direct involvement in the case. The petition was signed by more than 1.5 million people and the previously anonymous Shoesmith and Ward became the focus of unbridled rage. Shoesmith received death threats and Ward was forced to move out of her home in fear for her life.

In his book *Black Box Thinking*, Matthew Syed – who

describes the death of Baby P as 'one of the defining British tragedies of recent years' – offers a compelling take on the furious race to apportion blame that characterised the case.[59] 'To those on the receiving end, the experience felt like something close to the Salem witch trials. Something terrible had happened. The instinct was to ensure that something equally terrible happened to someone else. It was the blame game at its most vivid and destructive.'*

Syed reports that in the months that followed, many social workers resigned from their roles and the number of new recruits entering the profession dropped off dramatically. Inevitably, this led to a number of vacancies and served only to increase the already significant burden and strain being carried by those members of staff who remained. It cost a fortune too. One local authority reportedly spent £1.5 million on agency workers because they didn't have enough permanent staff to handle the workload. And the consequences didn't end there. A new culture of risk aversion meant that the number of children being removed from their families soared. In Haringey specifically, between 2008 and 2009, the number of care applications increased by more than 200 per cent.

'Defensiveness started to infiltrate every aspect of social work. Social workers became cautious about what they documented, in case it came back to destroy them. The bureaucratic paper trails got longer, but the words were no

---

* Shoesmith would later be awarded £680,00 for unfair dismissal whereas the Court of Appeal ruled Ward was not sacked unfairly.

longer about conveying information, they were about back covering. Precious information was concealed out of sheer terror for the consequences. The amount of activity devoted to protecting themselves from a future blood-letting undermined attention to the actual task of social work.'

People began to lose sight of the reasons why they were there. Front-line professionals tasked with the protection of children were forced to operate under greater pressure and scrutiny than ever before, and none of it made children any safer. I suspect that precisely the opposite is true. All for the need to find someone – anyone – to blame.

Social workers make mistakes. So do police officers. And on occasions, the consequences of those mistakes are catastrophic. There are individuals who were working for Haringey Council – and the Met Police – when Peter died who have doubtless faced some desperately uncomfortable questions about what they did and didn't do during the course of his short life. Mistakes might be made as a consequence of unprofessionalism or laziness; they might result from a lack of training; occasionally they are the result of downright malice (in which case they really aren't mistakes at all); but mostly police officers and social workers get things wrong because they are human. And none of them killed Baby P.

If you are really looking for the people to blame for Peter Connelly's death, then surely you need look no further than Tracey Connelly, Steven Barker and Jason Owen. They are certainly the only people in my sights, much as Marie-Thérèse Kouao and Carl Manning are for the murder of

Victoria Climbié. In the published photograph of Connelly, taken by the police after she was charged in relation to her son's death, she looks terrifying, with her sunken eyes and sullen face and the absence of any apparent trace of remorse. I want to call her a monster. But even as I acknowledge the instinct to label her, I sense that I am missing something – something important, albeit deeply uncomfortable. The fact is that Tracey Connelly was once Peter's age and as innocent as him. I don't believe that she was born evil; I don't believe anyone is. But that then begs the question, how did she become what she became?

When the journalist Andrew Anthony was asked to write a feature on Baby P for the *Observer* in August 2009, he went in search of Tracey Connelly's backstory.[60] Early in the piece, he writes: 'The savagery [apparent in the circumstances of Baby Peter's death] was the culmination of generations of abuse and dysfunction, a dreadful violation that was far from inevitable but that had none the less been incubating for decades.'

Anthony traced Connelly's mother, Mary O'Connor, and went to meet her. Describing her as a 'thin, hollowed-out woman', he pieced together the fragments of her early life. She was four days old when her own mother died. She was only five years old when her stepmother died. Her father was a violent man who beat her repeatedly. 'All I knew was violence,' Anthony records her saying. At the age of nine, she was sexually assaulted by a relative, and at the age of thirteen she ran away from home. She later married twice. Her second husband battered her.

Tracey was fathered by a different man, someone who had been convicted of sexually assaulting a child in the 1970s. When she was eighteen months old, she moved with her mother to London, leaving behind the violent husband and Connelly's older brother. Connelly was bullied as a child and was placed in a boarding school for children with behavioural difficulties. She was sixteen when she met her thirty-three-year-old future husband and the father of her four children. When that marriage came to an end, Steven Barker moved in. Nine months later, Baby Peter was dead.

These are the chilling stories of the intergenerational trans-ference of harm – of the recurrence of poverty and violence and chaos of every kind, inherited by parents and passed on to their children. They leave me with endless questions and a deep sense of conviction that we have got to do better than blame.

It is not enough to point fingers and pass judgements – about the lives of those who are broken beyond belief, or the actions of front-line public servants who have been charged with trying to mend them. We need to ask why it is hap-pening in the first place. We need to understand why some of the basic things that so many of us take for granted – not least a loving family and a safe place to call home – appear to be out of reach for some in our society. We need to support those who have never been parented in learning how to raise their children, and we must be ready and able to intervene at the earliest opportunity when things appear to be going wrong. We cannot just stand by and allow stories like those of Victoria Climbié and Peter Connelly to be told on repeat.

We maintain the illusion that all of this is somehow someone else's business, but the world really isn't made that way. As Martin Luther King once said, 'I cannot be what I ought to be until you are what you ought to be. We are not independent; we are interdependent.' And so it follows that we cannot simply leave it to the police – or to teachers and social workers – to try to repair these things. Because by the time one of them becomes involved, society has already failed.

XII. *Policing in 2020*

Alcohol abuse. Drug addiction. Domestic violence. Knife crime. Mental illness. Community–police relations. Public disorder. Terrorism. Sexual offences. Child abuse. Ten of the most urgent and overwhelming challenges of our time. And police officers stand in the front line of society's response to every single one of them.

I want you to see the things that they see. I also want you to understand that those police officers are operating under greater pressure and strain than at any other point in my lifetime. In fact, I would go so far as to say that these are the most challenging times for policing in this country since the end of the Second World War. That isn't some clumsy attempt at headline-grabbing hyperbole; it's just a simple statement of fact.

Crime is rising, and certainly crime of the most serious kinds. In 2017/18, there were 54,045 reported rapes in England and Wales, an increase of almost 13,000 compared with the year before.[61] And still four in every five rapes remain unreported to the police. In September 2019, the BBC reported that domestic murders in this country had surged to a five-year high,[62] and the fatal stabbings of young men on our streets continue unabated.

Demand on police time and resources is rising too, not least as a consequence of the enormous holes that have appeared in the delivery of every other front-line public service. Years of government cuts have had a crippling impact on the levels of care and support provided to the mentally ill, to young people, to vulnerable adults, to the unemployed and to those caught up in the criminal justice system. The cost of austerity has always been greatest for those least able to bear it, and policing remains the agency of both first and last resort for all of them.

But it's not just crime and demand. The job is becoming more complex too. Policing has always been complicated – nothing will ever be straightforward when people lie to you all the time – but it has become much more so than when I joined in the early 1990s. This is primarily due to astonishing advances in technology as both an enabler of crime and an accelerator of harm. Each year, the National Crime Agency publishes an assessment of the primary criminal threats facing the UK, and their 2019 report highlights the extent to which organised crime networks are using encryption, virtual currencies and the anonymity afforded by the dark web to further the trade in everything from drugs and guns to people.[63] For example, the NCA estimate that there are 2.88 million dark websites hosting the most extreme forms of child abuse and exploitation, including those that livestream hideous crimes via webcams. To date, the response of the big tech companies to all of this has been scandalously inadequate.

While crime, demand and complexity all continue to rise, so does the level of risk being faced by police officers out on the streets. We are now in a situation where more officers are being more seriously injured more frequently than at any time I can recall. Late on the evening of Thursday 15 August 2019, PC Andrew Harper of Thames Valley Police responded to reports of a suspected burglary in a rural part of Berkshire. He had just got out of his patrol car when he was hit by a suspect vehicle and dragged a significant distance along the road. He died of multiple injuries, less than a month after he had got married to Lissie, and a week before they were due to go on their honeymoon. Three teenagers were later charged with his murder. Lissie was a widow at the age of twenty-eight.

Andrew was killed in the same month that a North Yorkshire PC sustained complex leg fractures during an assault, a Met PC was very badly wounded in a machete attack, and a West Midlands PC was seriously injured after being run over by a suspected car thief. According to government statistics for 2018/19, 595 police officers in England and Wales are assaulted every week – 85 of them every single day.[64]

Each of these critical factors – crime, demand, complexity and risk – has been on the rise at a time when the number of police officers in this country has fallen to its lowest level in a generation. That collapse in numbers has come about as a consequence of conscious, deliberate government policy.

Politics and policing have always been uneasy bedfellows, better kept at a respectful, professional distance. Back at the start of my career, policing still held strongly to the fundamental notion of operational independence from political control. The idea was that politicians stuck to politics while police officers got on with policing.

Like the judiciary, the police service was always supposed to remain entirely separate from the executive branch of government, free from any form of undue political influence or interference. I was sworn in as a servant of the Crown, not of Parliament, and I was prohibited by law from taking part in any form of political campaigning. That was exactly as it should have been. But over the course of my working life, it seemed to me that the lines became increasingly blurred. While police officers tried, sometimes falteringly, to stay out of politics, increasingly politicians got stuck into policing. And the consequences have been incredibly damaging. The ideals of police transparency and accountability are fundamental in any open, democratic society – I am for more, not less. But it must be transparency and accountability free from political agendas. The role of policing in society is far too important to allow its capability or effectiveness to be undermined by partisan concerns.

In 2010, a new coalition government was formed, with Theresa May appointed as Home Secretary. From the outset, it was clear that the subject of police reform was high on the new regime's agenda. It ought not to have come as a surprise. As leader of the opposition, David Cameron had clearly signposted his views about what he called 'the last great unreformed public service'. In a keynote speech delivered as far back as January 2006, he had stated that 'It's time for a fundamental shake-up of policing in this country. You can't be tough on crime unless you're tough on police reform.'[65]

His concern appeared to be that substantial increases in police investment in preceding years had not been matched by commensurate improvements in police performance. Something needed to change. In fairness, his opinions were not entirely without foundation. The police service that I was part of during the 1990s and 2000s was lumbering, bureaucratic and frequently wasteful of public funds. While for the most part we were highly capable when it came to dealing with major incidents and serious crimes, the same could not be said for our handling of things like budgets, technology and infrastructure. In addition, we were still haunted by the label of 'institutional racism' and, in terms of both ethnicity and gender, we certainly didn't look much like the communities we served. Furthermore, during the latter years of the Labour government, policing had become mired in a hopeless public sector performance framework that actually did very little to make neighbourhoods and communities safer. In truth, there was a whole lot that needed to change.

Back in 2006, at the time of David Cameron's speech, if you had asked me whether I thought there was a need for reform in policing, I would have said an unequivocal yes. I would have said the same when the new government came to power in 2010 and I would still say the same now. Because I've never met a good copper who thinks policing is fine just as it is, that there's nothing left to improve upon. Whether it's supporting victims, catching perpetrators, safeguarding vulnerable people or managing dangerous offenders, there are always ways in which the job might be done better.

But nobody in any position of power asked me for my opinion. More importantly, I don't think they asked any of my colleagues either – and if they did, they can't have paid much attention to the answers they were given. Instead, politicians and their special advisers made the decision to chart a course of their own confrontational design. One of those advisers went so far as to describe himself and three of his colleagues as 'the four horsemen of the police reform apocalypse'.[66] In crude terms, it seemed that the government elected in 2010 regarded policing as a problem in need of fixing, and it became increasingly apparent that reform was something that was going to be done to policing – rather than *with* policing – whether policing liked it or not.

The first distinct change I noticed after the 2010 election was evident in the language being used by senior politicians. The prevailing narrative about policing rapidly became characterised by an extraordinary degree of hostility. The focus, particularly in the early years of the coalition, was relentlessly on the negative. The police were racist. The police were corrupt. The police were incompetent. The police could not be trusted to reform themselves.

The first problem with this approach was the simple fact that any substantial and effective transformation of policing requires a deep understanding of the job and its people. It is so much more an art than a science, a public service rather

than a private business. It is multifaceted and endlessly layered, as flawed and complex and demanding as life itself. And
it was apparent from the very beginning that the architects
of this period of police reform lacked a basic appreciation
of (and affection for) the institution they were dealing with.

On 29 June 2010, Theresa May gave her maiden speech
as Home Secretary. Addressing the annual conference of
the Association of Chief Police Officers, she offered her
unequivocal assessment of the role of the police in this
country. 'I couldn't be any clearer about your mission: it
isn't a thirty-point plan; it is to cut crime. No more, and no
less.'[67] The problem was that she was completely wrong. If
she had said that the *first* role of the police was to cut crime,
she would have been a little closer to the truth – after all,
the first of Sir Robert Peel's original Principles of Policing
states that 'the basic mission for which the police exist is to
prevent crime and disorder'. But even then she would have
been in danger of missing so much of what is important.
A huge proportion of what police officers deal with actually
has little, if anything, to do with crime – car crashes, missing
persons inquiries, people collapsed in the street, people
suffering from mental health crises standing on parapets,
non-suspicious deaths, natural disasters, house fires, peaceful
marches, major sporting events and all the rest. Each of these
involves the essential presence and participation of police
officers, directing traffic, searching scrubland, marshalling
crowds, administering CPR, clearing debris, giving instructions, holding out a hand to help. If the only role of the police
really was to cut crime, who would do everything else? It's

a question that might in fact be asked about the response to any number of things: if not the police, then who?

The second problem with the government's approach was that, so far as I am aware, the concept of police reform was never fully defined by the people responsible for it. In her June 2010 speech, Mrs May mentioned things like value for money, public accountability and getting officers back on the beat, but I can't recall ever seeing or hearing a coherent description of the supposed promised land that policing was being dragged towards. What we were faced with instead was a series of individual and frequently isolated changes that were imposed without any explanation or understanding of where they fitted into a larger plan. We had a collection of puzzle pieces, but no picture on the box to show how they were supposed to fit together.

Some of the changes introduced by the new government were downright provocative. Police authorities – the local bodies responsible for holding individual forces to account – were replaced by politically elected police and crime commissioners, given the power to hire and fire chief constables (further blurring the lines between operational independence and political control). For the first time ever, a civilian was appointed to the position of Her Majesty's Chief Inspector of Constabulary, given charge of the organisation responsible for reviewing and grading the performance of every force in England and Wales. In the past, that role had always been filled by a chief constable. In an added twist, the man given the job – Tom Winsor, a former rail industry regulator with no first-hand policing experience – was the author of an earlier, hugely controversial report that had recommended far-reaching reforms to police pay and conditions. Among other things, his work had prompted changes to police regulations that meant a new generation of officers would be working longer and paying higher contributions for a lesser pension than those who had joined before them. It doesn't require any great leap of the imagination to understand why this was so desperately unpopular among the policing rank and file.

Separately, the College of Policing was established as the independent professional body for the service, only to be viewed by many in the wider police family as no more than an extension of the Home Office and therefore just another mechanism for the delivery of politically motivated change. For the first time in modern policing history, it became possible to enter the service at the rank of superintendent, bypassing the years of front-line experience that had been foundational for every senior officer who had gone before. And so it went on, each new change introduced without any apparent reference to its place in a bigger picture. And if it's not clear where you're going, how on earth are you supposed to know if you've arrived?

Experienced police officers expressed serious concerns about the government's plans from the outset, but these were met largely with contempt on the part of the politicians and their allies, who presented them as evidence of a resistance to change that was, in and of itself, further proof of the need for reform.

All the while, the realities of austerity were biting. In the

years immediately following the 2010 election, the police service – in common with the rest of the public sector – faced
central government cuts on an unprecedented scale. Billions
of pounds were lost from local policing budgets, with far-
reaching and inevitable consequences.

A National Audit Office report published in September
2018 highlighted the fact that between 2010 and 2018, 44,000
officers and staff were lost from policing in England and
Wales.[68] That is a staggering number to lose in the space of
just eight years, and you cannot possibly expect to take that
many people (and that amount of money) out and expect
policing to carry on as if nothing has changed. To make the
challenge greater still, over the same period of time, the UK
population grew from just over 63 million to just over 66
million.

I was still serving for the vast majority of that period
and I witnessed first-hand all that was lost from policing
as a consequence of the government's actions. Patrol teams
lost officers, and with them part of the basic capability for
responding to emergencies. Neighbourhood policing was
decimated, impacting directly upon community engagement,
crime prevention and the gathering of critical street-level
intelligence. Policing became more reactive and less able to
address the underlying causes of crime, creating the potential
for a downward spiral of offending and a critical loss of confidence among local communities. A significant reduction
in the number of police community support officers (police
staff who patrol in uniform, providing visible reassurance to
local neighbourhoods) greatly exacerbated this reality.

We lost detectives from front-line investigative roles, with consequences for detection rates and the service provided to victims of crime. The loss of thousands of members of police staff resulted in a greater proportion of officer time being spent on administrative duties, as well as a reduction in key operational support in areas such as intelligence-gathering and analysis. We lost more than six hundred police stations, closed and sold off to the highest bidder. We lost vital specialist resources in the form of dogs, horses and helicopters, all proven to be highly effective in preventing and solving crime.

The Police Federation (the representative body for rank-and-file officers) warned the government repeatedly about the likely consequences of these cuts, but their concerns were dismissed. In her extraordinarily provocative 2015 speech to the Federation's annual conference, Theresa May declared: 'I have to tell you that this kind of scaremongering does nobody any good – it doesn't serve you, it doesn't serve the officers you represent, and it doesn't serve the public.'[69]

In the same speech, in words that would later come back to haunt her, she accused the Federation and its members of 'crying wolf', citing as evidence in support of her claims the fact that recorded crime was falling. This latter assertion became part of a mantra that senior politicians – the Home Secretary in particular – began to repeat on every occasion that the government's approach to policing was challenged or questioned. 'Crime is down, police reform is working,' we were all told.

The problem was that neither part of that statement was true.

I've already alluded to my concerns about the basic effect-iveness of the government's approach to police reform, and from the outset it was apparent that there were also a number of significant problems with their assertion that crime was falling. Beyond the recurrent dilemmas apparent with any set of published statistics is the fact that, as I have pointed out more than once already, police-recorded crime figures are likely to be an underestimate of the reality, particularly when it comes to some of the most serious types of offending – domestic violence, youth violence, sexual offences and the like. And if you don't know what the true levels of offending are, it is difficult to claim with any degree of confidence or certainty that crime is really going down. Beyond that, there is also the suggestion that the downward trends apparent in some recorded crime types had been established in the years before the new government came to power and the new era of police reform was ushered in.

In any case, the undeniable fact from 2018 onwards (per-haps even earlier) was that crime was in fact rising. Faced with this reality, Theresa May (who by then was prime minister) and Amber Rudd (her immediate successor as Home Secretary) tried to suggest that there was no connec-tion between rising crime and falling police numbers. But their claims defied both common sense and the operational experience of generations of police officers, my own included. In late 2018, a leaked Home Office report suggested that there was, in fact, a probable link between officer numbers and violent crime[70] – and the decision of the Met to redeploy hundreds of officers to deal specifically with the growing threat of knife crime seemed rather to reinforce the point.

The truth is that we had started to glimpse the long-term consequences of short-term cuts, and of the actions of a group of reckless police reformers who didn't properly understand who or what they were dealing with.

It is worth noting here that the combination of austerity and the government's approach to reform has also had a significant impact on the personal and professional lives of police officers and staff. As I look around me in policing now, I see many more good people operating under significantly more strain than ever before. You can see it in the sickness data, in the growing number of people off long-term with stress-related illnesses. You can see it in the internal staff survey numbers, in the suggestion that police morale is low and falling. You can see it in the early retirement figures, in the significant numbers of highly experienced officers leaving before their time is done, in search of a life less likely to break them. You can see it everywhere.

*

In October 2018, a report published by the Home Affairs Select Committee stated that police forces around the country were 'struggling to cope' with demand and warned of 'dire consequences' for public safety if the situation was left unaddressed.[71] In the same report, the Home Office was accused of a 'complete failure of leadership' when it came to policing. This latter assertion carried more than an echo of the National Audit Office report from the month before, which had stated that the Home Office had 'no overarching strategy for policing' in England and Wales. A complete failure of leadership and no semblance of a plan: it couldn't have been any more damning.

There is now a desperate need for substantial reinvestment in front-line policing in this country – for a complete reversal of the reckless neglect of austerity. In February 2019, the Police Federation published the results of an internal demand survey suggesting that almost 90 per cent of officers believed there weren't enough of them to be able to do their jobs properly.[72] The only surprise to me was that the figure wasn't closer to 100 per cent. There have since been some signs that politicians are beginning to wake up to these undeniable realities. In the summer of 2019, in one of his first announcements as Britain's newly appointed prime minister, Boris Johnson pledged to recruit 20,000 additional police officers in England and Wales. But while the basic headline was welcome, there could be no losing sight of the fact that this was a government scrambling desperately to undo harm entirely of its own making. And even if words eventually do become action, the truth is that 20,000 new officers won't even replace the basic number cut since 2010, and won't come anywhere close to addressing the combined losses of 44,000 officers and staff.

I want to make clear that these are not partisan views. I belong to no political party – I never have and I never will. My issue is with politics per se, and the concerns set out above are simply those associated with the government of the day. During my career, I encountered politicians of every persuasion who had an unerring ability to make policing even more difficult than it already was. Take the subject of stop and search, for example: an operational policing tactic that in recent years has been compromised in its effectiveness by politicians on both sides.

In a blog published by the *Spectator* in November 2018,[73] the former civil servant Alasdair Palmer spoke of the time he spent in the Home Office, working as a speech writer for Theresa May. He described an encounter with an unnamed special adviser who informed him that the Home Secretary wanted to make a parliamentary statement about the police use of stop and search. It was suggested to him that her motivation for doing so was in part political, arising from a recognition that stop and search had long been the subject of significant controversy, particularly within the black community.

> I was told that it would help the Home Secretary's standing with Afro-Caribbeans if she made a statement that was critical of the police's use of stop and search…
>
> The grounds would essentially be that the tool was racist, or at least used by the police in a racist way: the statistics demonstrated that you were six or seven times more likely to be stopped and searched if you were a member of an ethnic minority.

But when Palmer examined the evidence concerning police use of the tactic, apparent from research commissioned by the Home Office themselves, he found that perceptions were not borne out in reality:

...when you looked at who was available to be stopped
and searched when the police were actually stopping
and searching on the streets, the ethnic bias disappeared.
In fact, the police stopped slightly more white people
than they should have done if you looked solely at their
proportion of the street population.

The police, the Home Office research showed, did not
target particular areas for stop and search because they
wanted to stop and search people of a particular ethnic
group.

Palmer is evidently no apologist for the police use of
stop and search. His article makes clear that there are any
number of legitimate concerns that might be raised about
it, not least about the way in which searches are conducted.
Indeed, those are concerns I share. But he felt that the Home
Secretary's remarks ought to include a recognition of the
Home Office's own research findings. This was not to be.
According to Palmer, the special adviser reacted with fury
to the inclusion of the evidence, and it was omitted from
the final speech. The facts were ignored, because they failed
to suit the political purpose. And the overt politicisation of
stop and search contributed significantly towards massive
reductions in the use of the tactic throughout England and
Wales (a downward trend that, admittedly, had begun in
2012, following the previous year's riots, and in the face of
potential legal action against the police brought by the European Commission on Human Rights).

I believe that there is a direct connection between the fall in the police use of the power and the subsequent significant increase in the incidence of knife crime. It is not the only factor, of course – cuts to other front-line public services and the expansion of local drugs markets, for example, clearly have a part to play – but all my professional instincts tell me that reductions in police use of their powers have played a significant part. However, before we lay the blame exclusively at the door of a Conservative Home Secretary, we need to consider the approach taken to the same subject by a Labour candidate seeking election as Mayor of London.

Like Theresa May, Sadiq Khan understood that stop and search was a highly emotive issue for large sections of the community, and that the position he adopted in relation to it might consequently have an impact on people's voting choices. In an *Evening Standard* article published in September 2015, he is quoted as saying that if he was elected, he would 'do everything in [his] power to cut stop and search'. He appeared to have made a decision that this was a populist view likely to win him support among the electorate. But then he encountered reality. Having been elected mayor, and with knife crime soaring, Khan announced in the same London newspaper that the police would be 'significantly' increasing their use of stop and search in an attempt to stem the killings.

*

In the course of my policing life, I came across all sorts of politicians, on both local and national stages. Some of them were genuinely exceptional – dedicated public servants who cared deeply about their constituents and communities. But far too many of them left me with my head in my hands: frustrated, exasperated, disbelieving. I looked to Parliament, and beyond the women and men of real character, what I found there was a triumph of sound bite over substance, of expedience over conscience, of rhetoric over real understanding, of self-interest over service.

Most of them had little if any understanding of the realities of front-line policing. Almost none of them had any substantive first-hand experience of it (at the time of writing, there are only three serving Members of Parliament who have previously spent time as volunteer special constables). And when I did have an opportunity to speak to them about the critical operational challenges we were facing, it was almost impossible to get them to pay any attention. They seemed too preoccupied with the positioning of the camera, with the party line, with the next policy announcement or with the run-up to the next election. On those rare occasions when I was able to catch their interest, it was invariably only with a focus on the short-term. Most would put in an appearance on the day a teenager was murdered, but they would fade from view once the press had moved on and the real work had begun. And none of the intractable issues faced by policing is ever going to be fixed with that kind of short-sightedness. I tried to explain to them that where problems have been generations in the making, they might take generations to fix. But their attention seemed to wander, and the insights born of years of front-line policing experience were simply ignored.

It is worth pointing out that many of the concerns I'm

raising here about the impact of government policy on policing are being echoed in every other part of the public sector. Nurses and doctors are speaking out continually about the level of strain in the NHS. Lawyers are flagging up the state of the criminal justice system. Youth workers are talking about street violence and teachers about child and adolescent mental health. Prison officers are describing conditions in the nation's jails and food-bank volunteers are expressing deep concerns about basic poverty. And here's the thing: none of these people want us to vote for them. They are just dedicated public servants who want us to see what they see, to hear what they hear, to reach beyond the borders of our own comfortable existences and to understand how life can be.

*

It's not just politics that can make policing more difficult. Some of my encounters with politicians bear similarities with some of my encounters with members of the press. Over the years, I met a number of brilliant journalists – dedicated investigators committed to a genuine search for the truth. But I also encountered those whose approach I questioned. They shared with the politicians that same overwhelming (and desperately frustrating) preoccupation with the short-term. They asked the same limited questions in the aftermath of every murder and they appeared to have little interest in understanding what was actually driving the violence or what the answers to it might be.

If the demands of the electoral cycle narrowed the horizons of politicians, the demands of the news cycle did so to an even greater degree for reporters: the frantic race for the next headline in a fiercely competitive twenty-four-hour news age.

In the case of both politicians and journalists, there was a significant degree of self-interest involved: the former were trying to attract voters, while the latter were trying to attract readers and viewers. And in the case of the press, the content of the stories they wrote and told about policing appeared often to be less important than the potential for the accompanying headline to generate clicks.

Another characteristic they shared with their political counterparts was evident in the tone of the prevailing media narrative about policing; in their seemingly relentless preoccupation with the negative. The press certainly have a vital role to play in holding the police service to account. As I have suggested already, police officers should be expected to live up to higher standards than anyone else in society, and the press help keep us honest and true. I want reporters to question and challenge and be awkward when circumstances demand. I don't want them to let officers – or indeed the wider service – get away with anything. But there are other things that I want from them too, not least a far greater degree of balance – and accuracy – in the coverage afforded to policing. In the final years of my career, the job I love was relentlessly under attack in certain sections of the press. Often, it felt as though the only story being told was the one suggesting that we were inept or prejudiced or failing spectacularly in some other way. And while sometimes those things might have been true, what angered and frustrated me was the absence of any kind of counter-narrative.

Because most of the time the things that police officers do take my breath away. Every morning as a borough commander, I would scan the daily crime bulletin – a document that offered a summary of serious crimes committed and major incidents occurring in London during the preceding twenty-four-hour period – and every day there were remarkable tales to be told. But those didn't tend to be the policing stories that occupied the front pages of the nationals or the headlines on the news. Those were much more likely to be yet another story about individual corruption or institutional failure.

Of course there were occasions on which the press paused to acknowledge some of what is extraordinary about policing, usually in the wake of a terrorist attack or following the murder of an officer. But more often than not, within a day or two, normal service would be resumed and we would be left reading headlines confecting rage at the sight of armed officers smiling in public or their colleagues on emergency response teams daring to pause for a few minutes in the middle of a shift to grab a bite to eat. It would be laughable if it weren't so damaging – both to the standing of the service within the community and to the morale of individual officers and staff.

A few years ago, over a private cup of tea in a central London café, a prominent national journalist asked me a question that has stayed with me ever since: 'Who is standing up for policing in this country?'

It was clear from our conversation that he didn't think anyone was. The politicians were having a go at us, the press were having a go at us and the attacks from both seemed to be relentless. He told me that he had actually been given instructions by his editor to go out looking for stories that were 'difficult for policing'. In the face of all that, the voices of those wanting to offer a different perspective – one born of a love and respect for policing – were being almost completely drowned out. There was no semblance of balance in the story being told.

Every journalist who wants to write about policing needs first to spend time out on patrol with real police officers. And not just for an hour or two, but for a succession of lates and nights on a busy inner city division, in the places where real life is impossible to avoid.

As we enter the third decade of the twenty-first century, we are faced with the urgent need for a far-reaching national debate about policing in this country – one that involves not just Members of Parliament and members of the press, but every single one of us; one that poses a series of fundamental questions.

Firstly, and most importantly, we need to ask what we actually want the police service to be. Because the job of a police officer is about so much more than just crime. We need to decide whether we want their role to be defined primarily in terms of criminal justice outcomes (arrests, convictions and every other measure of enforcement activity), or whether we actually recognise and value their vital contribution to the much broader notion of community safety.

If we can reach a point of consensus about who they are supposed to be, we next need to consider what we want the police to do. And it will not be sufficient or in any way satisfactory to say that we want them to keep on doing everything – to continue plugging the gaps apparent across the public sector as the inevitable consequence of austerity. We need to determine where the role of policing begins and ends, and where other agencies – health, education, social care and the rest – need to step forward and take up the strain. In doing so, we need to reaffirm the simple truth that if everything is a priority, nothing is.

Having determined what their operational focus should be, we need to give them the resources they need – people, money, equipment, infrastructure, training – to be able to succeed. Effective policing is not of incidental significance to society; it is of fundamental importance to the ways in which we live our daily lives.

Finally, we need to appreciate with far greater clarity the unique set of personal and professional demands that police officers face. In the course of a normal lifetime, most of us will encounter serious trauma on no more than three or four occasions. In the course of a policing lifetime, officers are likely to do so on hundreds of occasions. Given that astonishing reality, we need to reconsider the level of support we provide them with, and in doing so, perhaps we also need to discover a renewed sense of deep appreciation for who they are and what they do.

In debating each of these things, we need to make sure that we listen and respond to the voices of genuine experience: to people who really know and understand what they're talking about, people driven not by the ambition for profit or power, but by the simple desire to see crime fall and neighbourhoods made safer. The fact is that these are the most challenging times for policing in this country that I have ever known: fewer officers and staff, with fewer resources, being asked to do a job that is more difficult, more demanding and frequently more dangerous than it has ever been before.

Conclusion: First and Second Things

Police officers are sometimes portrayed as cynical, world-weary types, ground down inevitably by years of dealing with the very worst that humanity has to throw at them. But I don't recognise that as a description of so many of the remarkable people I worked with during my career. I don't recognise it as a description of me either. I know that I have my scars, but I also have my hope. I had it when I started out as an idealistic twenty-something in search of adventure, wanting to change the world. I had it when I finished, a near-fifty-something, admittedly a little battered and bruised, but still wanting to change the world. And it remains with me now, not least in the form of a flat refusal to accept that the problems set out in the chapters of this book are impossible to solve. But if we really want to do something about the challenges facing us as a society, we need to start approaching them in a completely different way.

In 1942, the author C. S. Lewis published an essay entitled 'First and Second Things'.[74] At its heart is a simple proposition about basic priorities. For any given series of circumstances to turn out as well as they might, things need to be approached in the right order – and first things must always come first: 'You can't get second things by putting them first; you can get second things only by putting first things first. From which it would follow that the question, "What things are first?" is of concern not only to philosophers but to everyone.'

It is a question I have returned to often over the years. What things are first? And I wonder whether asking it now, in relation to the issues set out in these pages, might help us to understand what actually needs to be done about them.

Let's take the case of an eighteen-year-old boy who has been arrested on suspicion of murder at the scene of a fatal stabbing. His name is Billy Smith. He's not a real person, but his story and circumstances are hauntingly familiar, drawn very much from the real world.

While searching for evidence of his involvement in the crime – forensics, CCTV, eyewitness accounts and the rest – we also have an opportunity to go looking for clues that might help us to understand why he was drawn into violence in the first place. The chances are that we will begin with the fact that he's a known drug dealer.

Billy is a gang member who spends his days and nights dealing drugs. The boy he stabbed was a rival, a fellow dealer who had strayed onto his patch. Theirs was a dispute about territory; it was business. As these initial details become known, what is our response likely to be? What will be written in the headlines? What might be said on the floor of the House of Commons? I suspect that most of the talk will be about the things that are most obvious: drugs and gangs. We will be told that this is a crime problem – a police problem. And in the short-term at least, that would be true. Kids in gangs, armed with knives, dealing drugs are very much a police problem. But that diagnosis does little to help us in understanding, much less addressing, the reasons why Billy picked up a knife in the first place. Because in C. S. Lewis's terms, drugs and gangs are not the first thing. They are second things at best, and if we are serious about wanting to do something to prevent the senseless killings of teenage boys, we are going to have to look much deeper.

Crime is only ever a symptom of something else, and we need to ask why Billy started dealing drugs. Immediately we encounter an economic problem, one that has nothing whatsoever to do with crime. One of the reasons Billy began dealing was because he had no job and no prospect of getting one. He was flat broke. He spent his days on the streets, and selling drugs offered him the chance to make some easy money – far more than he would ever have made staying at home and claiming benefits. So we respond with the suggestion that the thing Billy really needs is meaningful employment, something that pays a decent wage. If we can secure that for him, we might stand some chance of setting his life on a different course. And to some extent we would be right – nothing stops a bullet like a job – but employment isn't the first thing either. We need to keep looking.

Billy is unemployed because he left school without any qualifications. That is an education problem. He struggled with the basics in a school that was unable to offer much in the way of vocational or creative education, or to teach the sorts of life skills that he so desperately needed to learn. The staff were overrun with the business of hitting targets for maths and English and so missed the things that Billy needed more. What he really needed was one-to-one attention and support, but the school was so short of resources that they couldn't afford to provide it. Inevitably, he got into trouble. It was relatively minor stuff at first, but it became more serious over time. He was excluded on a temporary basis after a fight with another pupil. He was excluded permanently when he was caught with a knife in his school bag. He didn't last long at the pupil referral unit either. So he spent his days sitting in stairwells and on street corners, falling under the spell of older boys, who groomed him for a life of crime. If only we had kept him in school, we might have kept him out of trouble.

But even education is not the first thing. We need to look beyond that, to the neighbourhood Billy grew up in, a stereotypical inner-city estate in the middle of a low-income, high-crime neighbourhood, characterised by generational poverty and joblessness and by the absence of any real sense that things will ever change. Billy has never travelled more than a couple of miles from his front door. He doesn't even know there's a river flowing through the middle of London. He believes, with some justification, that the streets beyond his immediate neighbourhood aren't safe for him. He started carrying a knife not because he ever planned to use it, but because he was afraid. Closer to home, his role models are toxic – dealers, robbers and moped thieves whose expectations seem limited to a binary choice between prison and mortuary.

But in surveying the disabling limitations of the small world he inhabits, we've still not arrived at the first thing. We need to get closer in. We need to find a way past his front door.

Billy has no dad. His biological father was gone by the time the boy was six months old – he was sentenced to three years inside for domestic violence and never showed his face again. Billy has no memory of him, and in any case wants nothing to do with him. Billy's mum is extraordinary, doing the very best she can in impossible circumstances, frequently working two jobs to provide for her family. But in a grim repetition of history, her last boyfriend beat her senseless and she's been unable to work for a while now. Billy has an older brother, but he's in prison after two earlier spells in a young offenders' institute. There's not much furniture in the flat and there's not much food in the fridge. If you took a moment to glance through Billy's Social Services file, you would see that his childhood has been marked by repeated trauma of almost every kind. It started in the weeks before he was born, when his dad kicked his mum in her swollen belly, and it continued throughout his early years. None of it was his fault, but it went a long way to defining who and what he became.

In his 2015 book *The Health Gap*, Michael Marmot suggests that, in responding to the great challenges of our age, we need to develop a much better understanding of 'the causes of the causes'.[75] He was talking primarily about health, but the principle applies equally to crime. You would be correct in suggesting that youth violence is, to some extent at least, being driven by the drugs trade. But we need to recognise that this is not the first thing. Unemployment and exclusion from education have a part to play, but they are second things. We need to identify and address the causes of the causes. The easiest thing in the world is to blame the police for rising violence or to blame schools for falling levels of educational attainment. But if we genuinely want to change the way things are, we are going to have to do a whole lot better than that.

*

All of us are searching for human connection – for relationships that matter and a place to call home. Some of us are blessed with those things from the very beginning; some of us have to search a little longer and a little further to find them. And some of us are like Billy.

I have no intention of diminishing the overwhelming seriousness of Billy's crimes, or his absolute responsibility for committing them. He has done something unimaginable and must now face the consequences of his actions. At the very least, he is going to have to spend a very long time in jail, and even then, there is nothing he or anyone else can do to bring his victim back. But while I'm not trying to give him an easy ride, I am trying to understand, recognising the truth that understanding is not the same as excusing. I am trying to find a way through it all and back to hope.

Not long ago, John Carnochan, co-founder of the Scottish Violence Reduction Unit, wrote to me: 'Humans are born connected and they stay connected. It's when disconnection occurs that issues arise. It's about being human and the soft human attributes that are anything but soft. Kindness is very difficult but, in the end, that's all there is. Gregory Boyle [Jesuit priest and founder of *Homeboy Industries*, a highly impactive American gang intervention programme] speaks of creating a circle of kinship that no one stands outside. The worst thing in the world is to be nothing to nobody.'

John's view is that 'whatever the question, the answer is relationships'. And he's right. Boys join gangs in search of relationships. Girls flee the country to join ISIS in search of a cause to believe in and a place to belong. The descent into drug and alcohol addiction so often begins with the fracturing of relationships – either in childhood or in later years. People remain in abusive homes in part because of the primal fear of being alone.

What Billy needs is to be something to somebody. He needs someone who believes in him. Old-fashioned though it may sound, what he needs more than anything else is someone who *loves* him – someone who is prepared to walk alongside him for as long as it takes to turn his life around. In the absence of biological family, it might be a teacher or a youth worker or a neighbour or a mentor. It might even be a police officer. Whoever it is, the thing that matters is that they are in it for the long haul – ready for it to be difficult and messy and heartbreaking at times, but unwilling to give up on him. In my experience, that is the only thing that will work.

I dare say some people will accuse me of being an idealist

here – of being unduly simplistic in my description of these things. But the truth is that any idealism I still possess after all my years at or close to the policing front line is tempered with a significant degree of pragmatism, not least given the uncomfortable realisation that so much of what we're doing to combat knife crime, domestic violence, human trafficking and the rest just isn't working. Something fundamentally different is required by way of a response to the problems we face as a society, but the desperate fact seems to be that we are either unable or unwilling to change our ways. I think there are four possible reasons for this.

First is the suspicion that it will take too long to put things right – time that we can't spare, time that we don't have. I've already made mention of the sort of short-termism that persists in politics and in the media, but it exists elsewhere too. We all seem to be in one great big hurry, relentless in our demands for life to be faster. Faster food, faster broadband, faster transport. Faster and faster and faster we go. And so we call for faster solutions to teenage stabbings and to every other kind of crime. Rather than actually trying to understand the reasons why boys carry knives or riots happen or addicts inject drugs, we resort endlessly to calls for more enforcement: additional powers for the police, greater prohibitions, tougher sanctions, longer jail sentences – the appearance of doing something without actually achieving anything of lasting worth. And if we make it a police problem, we can blame the police for not fixing it.

But how is that actually working out? Our prisons are overcrowded, the criminal justice system is in danger of collapse, the probation service is stumbling badly and police officers themselves are buckling under the loads they are being asked to carry. Resorting solely to enforcement as the solution to crime makes about as much sense as trying to put the roof on a house before you've dug the foundations. Or built any of the walls. Getting things right will certainly take time, but the irony is that repeatedly getting things wrong and needing to start over will take a whole lot longer.

The second reason for our failure to do what's required is the fear that we simply won't be able to afford it. The financial cost will be too high, particularly given the years of austerity that have blighted the country. Billions were lost from policing budgets in the years following the 2010 general election – the same in health, education and every other part of the public sector. We were told that we would have to make savings, that we needed to become more efficient, that we would have to do 'more with less'. But there is a world of difference between a saving and a cut, and the threshold between those two things was crossed a long time ago. As I have already suggested, there was undoubtedly scope for policing to become more efficient post-2010, but never at the expense of its fundamental effectiveness. We are now beginning to see the longer-term economic consequences of short-term (and short-sighted) cuts to front-line budgets. And it is going to end up costing us a fortune.

As violent crime rises, so do the costs to society. Take homicide, for example. Home Office figures published in July 2018[76] suggest that the financial cost of every murder is an astonishing £3.2 million. That figure is derived from estimates of three distinct forms of expenditure: costs in anticipation of crime (e.g. the cost of crime prevention measures such as the installation of CCTV); costs as a consequence of crime (e.g. the cost to the NHS of trying to save the victim's life); and costs in response to crime (e.g. the cost of the police murder investigation).

It might be an old truth, but prevention has always been better than cure, and not just in relation to crime. Inspector Michael Brown is the leading UK expert on policing and mental health, and he makes the same point regarding mental illness. He was the person who first suggested to me that the costs to society of treating mental ill health and its consequences are far greater than the costs would have been of helping people to stay well in the first place. Invariably, the price of getting it wrong ends up being much higher than the price of getting it right. The next time a politician questions whether we can afford to invest in policing or education or social care, our response must be that we cannot afford *not* to.

The third possible reason for our failings is the suspicion that doing what's required will turn out to be too difficult. Writing headlines is easy. Announcing yet another policy initiative is easy. Demanding that the police do more while the rest of us carry on regardless is easy too. Even paying out vast sums of money in an attempt to salve our consciences is easy in comparison to doing what actually needs to be done.

Two news stories that I read back in August 2017 illustrate the point perfectly. The first was about vehicle rentals – specifically, calls for a robust review of UK regulations concerning the hiring of vans. In response to the horrifying terrorist attacks that had taken place in mainland Europe in the preceding weeks, it was suggested that the authorities ought to make it more difficult for would-be mass murderers to secure the use of their preferred mode of transport (and destruction). The second story was about trains, revisiting an old proposal about introducing women-only carriages. It was a reaction to understandable concerns about a rising number of reported sexual assaults committed against female victims on public transport.

But as I read the two reports, I couldn't help feeling that – despite what might have been good intentions – both suggestions had completely missed the point. The fact is that the evils of international terrorism are not going to be overcome by some incidental tinkering with vehicle rental regulations. The evils of sexual assaults on trains are not going to be overcome by isolating potential victims in secure carriages. Here's the thing: it would undoubtedly be that little bit easier to introduce segregation on trains than it would be to resolve the generational ills of misogyny and male violence. It would be more straightforward to introduce some extra form-filling at car rental firms than it would be to unpick extremist ideologies that are beyond the comprehension of most of us. Terrorism and violence are difficult, and difficult demands far too much of us. Difficult takes far too long. Difficult costs far too much. Difficult is, well, just too difficult.

But that isn't good enough. There is an urgent need for us to rediscover our humanity – to be willing to do whatever it takes to save lives, to rescue slaves, to find lost children, to help the helpless, to defend the weak, to respond to every other aching need evident in society.

The fourth reason for our apparent reluctance to do the right thing is the fact that so much of what is described in this book takes place in a world beyond our view – beyond our experience and our understanding. Human beings tend to be most concerned about the things that have a direct impact on their daily lives. And so much of what has been written about here doesn't tend to affect people like me. If it did, perhaps I might be more inclined to do something about it.

A disproportionate number of London's young knife crime victims are black. They tend to be from poor families who live in troubled inner-city neighbourhoods. A huge proportion of the teenage victims of human trafficking come from similarly poor communities – towns like Rotherham, well off the Westminster track, or from Eastern Europe and beyond. They remain out of sight and out of mind. I can't help thinking that, had they been children of the establishment, the response to their plight would have been a very different one.

And so we need to cross that line between the world that is familiar to us and the one that remains so often beyond our view. We need to step beyond that blue-and-white cordon tape and stay for a while in the places where police officers spend their working lives.

*

It would be impossible to do the job of a police officer for any length of time and to remain untouched by the things you see. It would be easy to lapse into despair, were it not for the stubborn insistence of hope. I'm not prepared to give up on the victims of domestic violence and knife crime, of child abuse and human trafficking. I am not willing to accept that the immense harm done by drugs, alcohol and pornography is irreversible. I don't believe that the terrorists will ever win. And I haven't given up on Billy Smith, not by a long way.

But hope is not a passive thing; it demands action. We know what needs to be done; we just have to get on and do it. We need to understand that, while the cause could not be more urgent, nothing of lasting worth is going to be accomplished overnight. Human beings are slow-burning masterpieces, and it is going to take time to mend all that has been broken. It might actually take our lifetimes.

In the meantime, we need to recognise just how much it is costing us to get things wrong and to start spending our money in a completely different way: independent of political agendas, guaranteed for the long-term and focused relentlessly on the first things that must always come first.

To borrow from C. S. Lewis one last time, the problem is not that these things have been tried and found wanting; it is that they have been found difficult and left untried.

Epilogue: December 2020

At the start of 2020, as I was preparing for the publication of *Crossing the Line*, I was with the vast majority in having no idea that the world was about to change beyond all recognition. I had written about (and was getting ready to speak about) some of the greatest challenges facing us as a society – violence, addiction, extremism, racism and more – oblivious to the catastrophic public health tidal wave that was about to hit us.

So much has happened in the period since – so much that is relevant to the content of this book – that it seemed important to try to capture at least some of it for the paperback edition.

There are three things in particular that I want to focus on here – three things that have left their mark on me, not least as a consequence of the impact they have had on policing in this country. They are the coronavirus itself, the killing of George Floyd in America and the killing of Met Police Sergeant Matt Ratana in south London.

When I think about Covid-19, I think first about those who have died. I think about the sheer scale of the humanitarian calamity that has been playing out in real time all around us. The numbers are dizzying, almost too great to comprehend, and I have found myself trying to make sense of them in the context of other major disasters to have affected this country during my lifetime.

I think about Hillsborough, where ninety-six lives were lost. I think about the terrorist attacks in London on 7/7, with a death toll of fifty-two. I think about the 270 people who were murdered when a bomb exploded on an aeroplane in the skies over Lockerbie. I think about the fifty-one people who died when the *Marchioness* pleasure boat sank on the River Thames. I think about the capsizing of the *Herald of Free Enterprise* cross-channel ferry and of the 193 souls who drowned. Taken together, a total of 662 precious lives were lost in circumstances that no one of my generation is likely to forget. But 662 is not even close to the number of people we were losing daily in Britain when the virus was at its peak. During the spring and early summer, the grim repetition of the daily death tolls became almost too much to bear. Behind every number, there was a name. Behind every name, there was a family. Behind every family, there was a story. And none of those stories had happy endings.

Early in the year, some commentators were suggesting that coronavirus was 'the great leveller' – that it was no respecter of class or race or generation or gender. Any of us could catch it, they pointed out (after all, the Prime Minister himself had been hospitalised with it), and all of us would be affected by it. But from the beginning, there was something fundamental missing in their analysis.

While it was obviously true to say that anyone could catch it, the reality was (and is) that some individuals are much more vulnerable to the virus or more likely to be exposed to it than others: people with underlying health conditions, doctors and nurses and all those working in hospitals and care homes, paramedics, police officers, firefighters, people living in crowded accommodation with limited access to outside space, supermarket workers, bus drivers, cleaners – the list goes on. And, in far too many cases, woeful shortfalls in the availability of sufficient or adequate personal protective equipment made an incredibly difficult situation substantially more dangerous.

While it was also true to say that all of us would be affected by it, when viewed across society as a whole, it is clear that the impact of coronavirus has been much greater for some than others: for the poor, the vulnerable, the marginalised, the elderly, the lonely, single parents, those already suffering with mental ill health conditions, those without a secure income; those already contending with every possible form of disadvantage. As with austerity, it seems apparent that the costs and consequences of Covid are greatest for those least able to bear them.

Among those most adversely affected by the wider consequences of the virus are the victims and survivors of domestic violence (DV). In Chapter IV, I described DV as 'a disease of pandemic proportions' – a phrase written long before the Covid realities of 2020 became apparent – and it is a description I stand by now. Coronavirus has only made things worse.

During the first three weeks of the first national lockdown, the number of DV murders in this country more than trebled. In evidence given to the Home Affairs Select Committee on 15 April, Dame Vera Baird QC, the Victims' Commissioner for England & Wales, stated that there had been at least sixteen DV-related murders of women and children between 23 March and 12 April 2020. This compared with an average of five over the same period during the preceding ten years.[77]

According to a BBC News report published in July, more than 40,000 phone calls were made to the National Domestic Abuse Helpline during the first three months of lockdown.[78] Most of the callers were women. In June 2020, contact with the helpline was almost 80 per cent higher than normal and, as lockdown restrictions began to ease, there was a significant rise in the number of women seeking places in refuges.

The findings of a separate BBC *Panorama* investigation, broadcast in August 2020, suggested that two thirds of women trapped in abusive relationships had suffered an increase in violence at the hands of their partners since the pandemic had begun.[79] To make things even worse, three quarters of them stated that lockdown had made it harder for them to consider the possibility of escape. DV remains a hidden crime, so often taking place behind closed doors. When those doors are not only closed but locked, the risks faced by those living behind them increase substantially.

During the first seven weeks of lockdown, *Panorama* estimated that UK police forces were receiving a DV-related call every thirty seconds. And those are just the cases that the police were told about.

At this point, it is important to emphasise that the virus itself is not to blame for the surge in domestic violence. If my years in policing taught me anything, it is that the only cause of male violence is violent men, and there has never been any excuse for it. What the pandemic did do was place significant additional pressure on the domestic settings in which violence and other forms of abuse were already happening. Women and children died as a consequence.

As I write now, in December 2020, the news bulletins are dominated by headlines and hope-filled stories about the successful development of several coronavirus vaccines. There is a real possibility that, less than a year after the first cases were reported in this country, a life-saving answer to the virus might have been found. It is extraordinary to see what human beings can achieve when the will, the urgency, the expertise and the investment are all in place. If only the same were true of society's response to DV. The end of one pandemic may be in sight, but the other continues. Domestic violence remains the single greatest cause of harm in society.

The victims and survivors of DV are not the only ones to have been placed at significantly greater risk because of the virus. Research published by the NSPCC suggests that the circumstances of the pandemic also heightened the vulnerability of children to multiple forms of abuse – including online abuse, abuse within the home, criminal exploitation and sexual exploitation.[80] According to the NSPCC this was due, in part, to the increase in 'stressors' apparent in the lives of parents and carers (lockdown, cramped living conditions, financial instability and so on) and, in part, to the loss of 'normal' safeguards in the lives of those most at risk (interaction with extended social networks, school attendance and the like). As with DV, these are so often victims without voices, trying to survive in circumstances that most of us can't even begin to imagine. And police officers stand first in line to respond to them all.

*

Significant and deeply alarming escalations in some of the most serious forms of crime – impacting the lives of some of the most vulnerable people in society – have not been the only direct consequence of Covid for policing. Crime is at least familiar to police officers. They have some idea of how best to respond to it. They have the mistakes and the lessons of the past to draw on. They have the wisdom and experience of their colleagues to lean on. But in March 2020, they were pitched into the frontline of the greatest public health emergency of our lifetimes. And there was no handbook for that.

Imperfect, untested legislation was drafted in a hurry. Incomplete, inadequate guidance was rushed out. Government messaging seemed repeatedly to confuse rather than clarify. A slogan does not a strategy make but, in the early weeks of lockdown, it was hard to escape the conclusion that the government was relying far more heavily on the former than the latter. At times, they seemed to be making it up as they went along and the police, like the rest of us, were expected to make sense of it all. Unlike the rest of us though, officers were also expected to interpret and apply the legislation and guidance out on the streets. Developing an effective law enforcement response to an unprecedented public health emergency was never going to be straightforward, but an already challenging job was made immeasurably more so by the determination, readily apparent in certain sections of the media, to find fault in almost everything that police officers did.

When it came to the policing of the pandemic, the early press headlines focused almost exclusively on the negative: on isolated instances of individual officers misinterpreting or over-reaching their new powers. The reports broadcast and published were about supermarket aisles being patrolled, shopping bags being searched, picnics being disrupted and police drones being flown over rural beauty spots. Many of these stories were inaccurate, though that didn't seem to trouble the consciences of those who were responsible for telling them. All the while, journalists were paying little attention to accounts of police officers being coughed on, bitten and spat at by suspects claiming to have the virus. Or to tales of PCs visiting elderly residents isolating in their homes, doing their shopping and filling their fridges. Or to stories of the thousands of their colleagues who were simply getting on with their jobs, trying to do their best in unparalleled circumstances, out and about on the streets, risking their own health and that of their loved ones. When it comes to policing, bad news travels much faster and further than good news. And, on the occasions when it turns out that the original reports were misleading or false, the damage has already been done. The relentless criticism was deeply demoralising.

One remarkable element of the policing and wider emergency services response to Covid that has been overlooked by many sections of the media is the work of the Pandemic Multi-Agency Response Teams (PMART). PMART officers and their colleagues from the Fire Service and the NHS were responsible for responding to every non-hospital coronavirus death. It has always been the responsibility of the police to deal with 'sudden deaths' in the community – to attend the location, to assess whether there are any suspicious circumstances, to comfort a grieving family, to liaise with the coroner – but never in the midst of a global pandemic. Never with people dying in such numbers. Never in the face of such enormous personal risks.

Up and down the country, Pandemic Multi-Agency Response Teams were formed rapidly to address overwhelming need. In London, the first PMART shift was on 31 March 2020. Mixed crews made up of police officers, firefighters and health professionals were recruited, trained and deployed in a matter of days. They attended every scene of a Covid-related death. Their role was to liaise with any ambulance crew already there, to confirm that life had been pronounced extinct, to establish the circumstances in which the person had died, to carefully prepare the body for safe removal and, perhaps most importantly of all, to catch a family falling in their sorrow. On their busiest day in the spring of 2020, London's PMART crews were called out on forty-two separate occasions.

Not long after that most demanding of days, I spoke at length to one of the PMART PCs – I'll call him Pete – to find out more about the work that they were doing. As with every other member of his new team, he had set aside his day job in order to take his place in one of the cars.

Pete had lost his own father just the year before, and it was the memory of his dad that he carried with him as he prepared to respond to his first PMART call. He wondered how it might affect him, how he might feel. Because, beneath the uniform, police officers are people just like you and me. And I think we forget that sometimes. Pete described to me the protective clothing that he and the rest of the team were required to put on each time they were deployed – a full hazmat suit, gloves, mask and goggles. He described the way in which the kit acted not just as a physical barrier, but as an emotional one too. He described one of his earliest calls: to a husband who had died; to a wife who was now all alone. He told me about the eventual arrival of members of her family, who came to the front of the house, but no further. Because that was as close as the virus would allow them. There were no comforting embraces – there was no physical contact of any kind. The one thing a widow most needed was the one thing she was denied. Similar scenes were unfolding up and down the country, multiple times, every single day.

After speaking to Pete, I also spoke to one of the PMART sergeants. I'll call him Andy. The first thing Andy wanted to tell me was just how proud he was of the people he was working alongside. He talked about the sense of purpose he felt in what they were doing – in their contribution to an extraordinary national effort. Dealing with dead bodies was perhaps the most immediate and obviously difficult part of their role but, for Andy, it was dealing with the families that represented the greatest responsibility. Sometimes police officers and their emergency services colleagues are the only ones with shoulders strong enough to bear the full weight of another's grief.

The youngest coronavirus victim that Andy dealt with was twenty-one. The oldest was ninety-seven. And every contact leaves a trace. The older man reminded him of his own grandmother who was living in a nursing home at the time and as vulnerable as can be. So often, the stories of strangers have echoes in tales of our own. 'It's a grim job, there's no two ways about it,' he told me. 'But it matters.'

Like every police officer, I suspect that Pete and Andy long ago lost count of the number of dead bodies they've seen over the course of their careers, but Pete told me that the PMART role was unlike any other he had taken on before. At the end of every shift, he would make his way home to his wife and two young children, carrying with him the memories of faces and places he will never forget, together with the unspoken fear that, in the course of performing his duties, he might have caught the virus too.

I have often heard it suggested that policing is an extra-ordinary job done by ordinary people. But it's a description that has never quite seemed right to me. It's the 'ordinary' bit that doesn't add up. When I look back now and think of the best of the women and men I served alongside, I recognise that, in order to be able to do the job of a police officer – and to do it well – you need to be extraordinary in the first place.

One of the many enduring reasons why police officers need to be extraordinary is in order to withstand the relentless criticism that they are so often subjected to. When it comes to their work, officers frequently feel damned whatever they do, and that sense has never been more apparent than during the policing of the pandemic. It's not just the barrage of media criticism and the verbal abuse from ordinary members of the public, it's the physical violence too. During the first three months of the first lockdown, there was a 21 per cent increase in the number of assaults on police officers in this country.

Writing now, nine months on from the beginning of that first lockdown, officers continue to be hammered by some observers for being too draconian, too heavy-handed in their enforcement of Covid-related regulations, while simultaneously being vilified by others for not being robust enough. Sometimes it feels as though you just can't win. Perhaps it was ever thus, but there is no doubt in my mind that front line officers are feeling the burden and the tension more now than ever before.

Coronavirus undoubtedly presented the greatest policing challenge of 2020, but it was far from being the only one.

On 25 May 2020, a black citizen was killed by a white police officer on the streets of Minneapolis. I found the widely shared video footage of the last few minutes of George Floyd's life too distressing to watch, but the broader circumstances and consequences of his death were unavoidable. They were – and they remain – too important to turn away from.

The greatest duty and privilege that any police officer could ever have is to save the life of another human being. The killing of George Floyd represents a betrayal of everything I have ever believed in as a person and everything I stood for as a police officer. I have no doubt that every decent copper would say the same. It seems to me that the only reasonable, rational response to his death is one of righteous anger and an urgent cry for real change.

Though his killing was a particular American tragedy, it rapidly became apparent that his story was universal, as marches and demonstrations began to gather all around the world. In Britain, his death assumed huge significance, not least because the manner in which he died seemed to carry a thousand echoes of the experience of black people in this country: echoes of their experience of policing; echoes of their experience of wider society; echoes of history; echoes of the subjects I was trying to write about in Chapter VII.

As social media lit up and the streets began to fill with protestors, I determined to stop and listen to what people were saying – recognising and reaffirming the simple truth that listening is the beginning of hearing, hearing is the beginning of understanding, and understanding is the beginning of change. When it comes to black history and black experience, I have nothing to teach and everything to learn.

Alongside the passionate and insistent cries of 'black lives matter', these are some of the things I heard people say:

'The police are institutionally racist.'

'They always have been and they always will be.'

'Nothing changed after the Scarman Report in the 1980s.'

'Nothing changed after the Stephen Lawrence Report in the 1990s.'

'Nothing ever changes.'

'Black communities are deliberately targeted by the police.'

'Black people are disproportionately more likely to be stopped and searched by the police.'

'Black people are disproportionately more likely to be tasered by the police.'

'Black people are disproportionately more likely to die in the back of a police van or in a police cell.'

'No police officer has ever been convicted of any crime following the death of a black person in custody.'

'Black lives are cheap.'

'All coppers are bastards.'

'Defund the police.'

As a fiercely proud former copper, it was a lot to take in. But in a world where shouting with our fingers in our ears is fast becoming the dominant mode of communication, it seems more important than ever to pause – for as long as is necessary – to listen to, and seek to understand, the stories of those whose lived experience is different from my own.

What follows is my attempt to respond to some of what I've heard and to try to explain some of what I hope I'm beginning to understand – beginning with that restless rallying call of recent times: 'black lives matter'.

Without wanting to lose myself immediately in semantics,

it seems to me that there is a distinction to be drawn between *'Black Lives Matter'* (a broad global movement) and *'black lives matter'* (a statement of personal belief). It's an important distinction because I'm not yet sure that I know and understand enough about the aims and intentions of every participant in the global movement to be able to articulate a properly rounded view about it. But when it comes to the statement of personal belief, I am all in. It is something I believe with every fibre of my being. Black lives matter.

To respond to that assertion by insisting that 'all lives matter' is to miss the point. White lives have always mattered, and no one is seriously suggesting that they now need to matter less. The point is that black lives need to start mattering a whole lot more than they have done in the past. The fact is that black people in this country (and across the globe) have, for generations, faced overwhelming forms of injustice and inequality that are both societal and systemic. In trying to understand what that means in practical terms, we might begin with the inescapable fact that black people are disproportionately more likely to die from Coronavirus and work our way back from there. Because black people in this country are also disproportionately more likely to be born into poor households, to live in high-crime neighbourhoods, to be excluded from education, to be unemployed, to suffer with mental ill health, to end up in prison. And so it goes on. This is the 'fundamentally unjust system' described by my friend in Chapter VII.

Which brings me to the much-debated question of 'institutional racism'. In considering it here, it might make sense to start with my conclusion. I have come to believe that the police service in this country is institutionally racist. Which, given my professional background, might well be the last thing you expected me to say. But before you jump to either congratulate or condemn me for reaching such a determination, let me explain how I got there. What I want to say has nothing to do with virtue signalling or political correctness. It has everything to do with trying to understand history and attempting to follow the evidence.

I was almost seven years into my policing career when the Stephen Lawrence Inquiry concluded that the Metropolitan Police Service was 'institutionally racist'. I remember it like it was yesterday. I felt bewildered, defensive and genuinely upset. I know that thousands of my colleagues were feeling the same way. I didn't think that I was a racist and I couldn't for the life of me understand why the inquiry panel appeared to be telling me that I was. It has taken me years to understand that that wasn't what they were doing at all; to realise they were actually talking about something much bigger than me, something much bigger even than policing, something built into the foundations and framework of our society.

Part of the difficulty when it comes to any debate about institutional racism is the lack of consistent and shared understanding of what the term actually means. Some use it to characterise the behaviour and impact of whole organisations, while others use it to describe the conduct of the individuals who make up those organisations, and there are any number of variations beyond those two perspectives. So I want to be absolutely clear about what I mean by it.

I don't think that all police officers are racist. I don't think that most police officers are racist. Completely the opposite in fact. In more than twenty-five years as an officer, I only encountered one overt display of racism from one of my colleagues, and that was almost thirty years ago. I think that the majority of police officers are anything but racist and that they were as horrified by the killing of George Floyd as the rest of us. I think they would stand shoulder-to-shoulder with the American police chief (@ChiefDavidRoddy) who, two days after George Floyd was killed, posted the following comments on Twitter:

> There is no need to see more video. There [is] no need to wait to see how 'it plays out'. There is no need to put a knee on someone's neck for NINE minutes. There IS a need to DO something. If you wear a badge and you don't have an issue with this... turn it in.

The overwhelming majority of police officers care passionately about injustice. It's why they joined the police in the first place.

Institutional racism is not primarily about individuals, it is about the system that they are a part of. That we are all a part of. That is not to absolve individuals of their personal responsibilities (to stand up for what is right; to speak out against what is wrong; to be active participants in change), it is simply to recognise that there is something going on here that is far bigger than any one of us.

Another difficulty with any discussion about institutional

racism is the fact that we seem to be living in an increasingly binary world, where you are either for me or you are against me and there is nothing in between. As a consequence, we are in danger of losing the middle ground: a safe space in which we are free to disagree and still remain friends. It's either my view or the wrong view, and that's all there is. The debate about 'taking the knee' offers a typical example. On one side of the invisible divide, those who kneel are labelled as Marxists. On the other, those who don't are called racists. Each camp judges and defines the other accordingly. It appears that there is no room for those who might want to kneel in prayer or penitence, or in a gesture of solidarity with those who have suffered; or for those who might choose to stand rather than kneel, but who are no less passionate about or committed to a righteous cause.

I think I understand therefore why senior police officers often appear reluctant to accept the label of 'institutional racism'. It is because of the fear that many of us, police officers included, will never get beyond the headline. We will read it, misunderstand its intended meaning, and respond accordingly. In a world that is moving far too fast, it is difficult to persuade people to slow down and properly examine the consequences of several hundred years of structural inequality. If policing is institutionally racist it is because that is the nature of the society we have made. The same is true of government, of the BBC, of the Church of England and of every other major institution in this country. As Glennon Doyle suggests in her remarkable book *Untamed*, it is in the air we breathe.[81]

That is not to suggest that I am trying to give policing some kind of 'pass' here (the 'we're no worse than the rest of them' defence has always been a terrible one to advance, particularly for the police service). Somehow, we need to find a way to get beyond the recurring (and depressing) cycle of accusation and denial. Policing has changed immeasurably for the better since I joined in 1992, but on the issue of race – and on many others besides – it still has a long way to go. And the nature of the role that policing occupies in society and the unique set of powers and responsibilities that police officers have been given means that our expectations of them ought to remain higher than they are of anyone else. The fact is that policing in this country should be at the forefront of challenge and change, especially when it comes to institutional racism. This is not about taking sides in an argument (and it therefore presents no threat to the precious notion of police impartiality), it is about doing the right thing. This is not a political issue. It is a justice issue. And, as Dr King wrote in his famous 'Letter from Birmingham Jail', 'Injustice anywhere is a threat to justice everywhere'.

My concern about the current debate regarding racial injustice in this country is not that it has gone too far, but that it has not gone nearly far enough. My fear is that time passes and much of the world grows increasingly impatient to move on when nothing of real and lasting substance has actually changed. This is about so much more than pulling down statues.

*

So what about the suggestion that we should 'defund the police'?

As with 'institutional racism', it is one of those phrases that is open to more than one interpretation. It has a particular meaning in an American context (relating to the ways in which US policing is organised and funded), that doesn't necessarily apply in this country. For example, US Law Enforcement is much more decentralised than in Britain and, unlike here, American policing has no national oversight body. Then there is the fact that many of those in positions of operational leadership (including sheriffs and even some police chiefs) are elected rather than appointed. But the wider implications of the term are certainly deserving of consideration.

In its broadest sense, 'defund the police' is in fact a fairly accurate description of exactly what the UK government did for the best part of a decade, from 2010 onwards. As I described in Chapter XII, between 2010 and 2018, 44,000 officers and staff were cut from policing in England and Wales and billions of pounds were taken from policing budgets. The consequences of these political decisions have been so devastating that the current government has spent much of the time since trying desperately to find ways of undoing the damage caused by their predecessors. In Chapter VII, I made mention of the harm done to neighbourhood policing as a consequence of the cuts. The loss of local relationships between police officers and members of the communities they serve has been one of the primary drivers of the current, undeniable 'trust deficit' that exists between the police service and the black community in particular. One of the legacies of the killing of George Floyd must therefore be an urgent renewal of demands for substantial reinvestment in community policing. All that is good about policing starts in local neighbourhoods.

Beyond the abject failures of recent government policy, there is another, more specific, context in which the term 'defund the police' might be used. There is an enormous amount of current evidence to suggest that police officers are currently being asked to perform many roles in society that should always have remained the responsibility of others. The provision of critical mental healthcare is perhaps the most obvious example to cite here. In Chapter VI, I described the woeful state of current mental health provision in this country: the inadequacy of the treatment and support offered to incredibly vulnerable people, and the fact that it is police officers who are so often left to pick up the pieces that other agencies have left behind. In this context, the 'defund the police' argument is that money should be taken away from policing and invested in the provision of better mental healthcare. The indisputable logic is that if we do a better job of helping people to remain well, there would be far less need for the police to become involved in the first place. And, in principle, every police officer I have known would agree.

The difficulty with this view comes at the point where it collides with reality, and with the realities of austerity in particular. Every part of the public sector in this country has already been cut to the bone. There is nothing left to take.

*

Someone once suggested that 'a copper's lot is not a happy one', but I would beg to disagree. My days as a police officer were some of the happiest of my life. But a copper's lot is certainly not an easy one. At times, it can seem like an impossible one.

Overwhelmingly, the Black Lives Matter protests of 2020 were peaceful. But on Saturday 6 June 2020, police officers in central London came under attack from a lawless minority of demonstrators claiming to represent the anti-racist BLM cause. The following weekend, as the far right gathered in counter-protest on the same London streets, police officers were attacked by racists. Sometimes, a copper's lot is to face hatred and recrimination from every side.

During late spring and early summer, there was one slogan that appeared on an endless succession of demonstrators' placards and banners. Variations of it were spray-painted on vehicles and graffitied on walls. This is what it said: 'All coppers are bastards.'

It is a horrible phrase, one born of both ignorance and malice. It bothers me for a whole host of reasons, the most obvious being that it simply isn't true. To suggest that all coppers are bastards is to be complicit in nothing more than a lazy lie – a dull stereotype that has no basis in evidence or fact. (If you were to say to me that *some* coppers are bastards, I would agree with you. I've met a handful of them in my time and they had no place in policing.)

The suggestion that 'all coppers are bastards' also bothers me because of the inevitable and substantial harm that it does to policing. Language matters. In recent years, some politicians and elements of the press have been guilty of repeatedly demonising the police: telling us that they are racist, corrupt and incompetent. Telling us, in effect, that they are bastards. During the June 2020 protests, I saw clear evidence of prominent journalists and comment-ators using extraordinarily inflammatory language about policing and even appearing to take delight in the sight of a mounted officer falling from her horse. The officer suffered a broken collarbone, broken ribs and a punctured lung. When that kind of horror story becomes an apparent cause for rejoicing, it leaves me wondering what on earth we are becoming as a society. Language matters, because it has real consequences in the real world. And when those in positions of power and influence consistently denigrate policing, they put officers' safety at risk. They put officers' lives at risk.

But 'all coppers are bastards' is not just damaging to poli-cing. It is also damaging to wider society. As I pointed out in Chapter VII, policing in this country is founded on the notion of consent, on the basis of a partnership established between the public and the police. We are them and they are us. It means that, in the end, what damages policing damages all of us. The police are not the enemy here. Racism is. Hatred and injustice and poverty and inequality are the things we should be fighting. If you are truly com-mitted to tackling those things, and if you sincerely want better policing, you will find no greater allies in your cause than good police officers. Because they want exactly the same.

More than anything, the accusation that all coppers are bastards bothers me because it requires a conscious denial of every extraordinary thing that any of them has done: of the lives they have saved, the lost they have found, the vulnerable they have protected, the dangers they have confronted. The police officers stopping and searching teenagers out on the streets are the same police officers fighting to save the lives of teenagers when they've been stabbed. They're not different people. To suggest that all of them are bastards demands that we ignore every act of humanity and heroism that any of them has performed. And it demands that we ignore the sacrifice of those officers who have paid the greatest price of all.

Most give all they can. Some give all they have. On Thursday 24 September 2020, Sergeant Matiu Ratana – known to all as Matt – went to work and didn't come home. He was on duty at the Croydon custody centre in south London when he was shot in the chest. He didn't stand a chance.

I never had the privilege of serving alongside him, but by all accounts Matt was a wonderful, larger-than-life character: a proud Kiwi of Maori heritage, passionate about rugby, passionate about policing and loved by all who knew him. In any other year, we would have gathered in our thousands – police and public side by side – to line the streets and pay our respects as his funeral cortege passed by. But the virus made that impossible, and so we paused for a while in the quietness of our own homes to watch the livestream of the service. The Commissioner's voice cracked as she paid tribute to him. The legendary All Black Zinzan Brooke joined his friends in performing a final haka in his honour. And we said goodbye to one of our own.

Okioki i te rangimarie, as Matt's ancestors might say. Rest in peace.

The murder of Sergeant Ratana served as a shattering reminder to all of us of the risks that every police officer faces. For a day or two at least, we stopped calling them bastards and remembered to be grateful for their courage and their sacrifice.

But from a police officer's point of view, it rarely takes long for what feels like normal service to be resumed. Mostly, it remains deeply unfashionable to express admiration or appreciation for the women and men who stand on the thin blue line.

On Friday 8 May 2020, the nation marked the seventy-fifth anniversary of VE Day. The main BBC broadcast that evening included a timely and beautiful musical tribute to key workers and members of the emergency services. Except that the police weren't featured in it. There were teachers and nurses, members of the armed forces and farmers, train drivers and shop workers, ambulance crews and firefighters, pharmacists and vets, doctors, bin men and posties. But no police officers. It was an extraordinary omission for the BBC to make and it left me trying to understand why we so often seem to feel differently about police officers when compared with other public servants, and members of the other emergency services in particular.

Nurses help people. And we love them for it.

Doctors help people. And we love them for it.

Firefighters help people. And we love them for it.

Paramedics help people. And we love them for it.

Police officers help people too, but somehow we don't quite seem to feel the same way about them. If you ask most coppers why they joined, they will tell you that it was because they wanted to help people. But they would be the first to acknowledge that helping people is not all they do. Sometimes they stop people; they pursue people; they challenge people; they issue fines for Covid breaches; they search people; they arrest people; sometimes they use force to do some of those things; and, as I am always at pains to acknowledge, they don't always get it right.

Perhaps it is for some combination of those reasons that we find them harder to love. Because there is a part of policing that is rough – involving the kind of violence, trauma, chaos and catastrophe that most of us would prefer never to have to think about, much less confront.

Please don't misunderstand me. I am not expecting people to suddenly start expressing their unquestioning support for policing in this country. Neither am I asking people to be any less demanding of the officers who do the job. All that I am asking – all that any police officer is asking – is for some semblance of balance: a recognition that most coppers aren't bastards, that they do a job that most of us couldn't or wouldn't do; a realisation that, one day, we might just need them and that they won't hesitate to come when we call; an understanding of the fact that, every day, they are the ones who are crossing the line, willing to face whatever horror and harm lies on the other side of that strip of blue and white tape.

Acknowledgements

Writing is a solitary undertaking that in my experience depends almost entirely on the wisdom, encouragement and love of a whole host of other people. And I want to say thank you to them.

To Rose Fitzpatrick and Gavin Hales, who read the full first draft of this book and offered me all manner of sound advice and guidance.

To the brilliant people who contributed their knowledge and experience to specific chapters: Mick Urwin, Patrick Navin, Jason Kew, Neil Woods, Gemma Jackson, John Carnochan, Dr Charlie Howard, Malcolm Stevens, Stan Gilmour, Michael Brown, Duwayne Brooks, Sheldon Thomas, Ben Lindsay.

To the remarkable James Seymour, Erwin James and Will Johnson for the immense privilege of telling some of their stories in these pages.

To the best agent in the business, Laura Williams.

To Paul Murphy, who published *Blue* and who commissioned this book.

To Jenny Lord, Ellie Freedman, Izzy Everington, Sarah

Benton, Cait Davies, Leanne Oliver, Maggy Park, Tom Noble, Luke Bird and every other lovely person at Weidenfeld & Nicolson.

Most importantly of all, to Bear, Jessie, Charlie and Emily. You are all as beautiful as can be and the four best things that ever happened to me. I love you.

Notes

II. *Drunk and Incapable*

1 http://www.ias.org.uk/Alcohol-knowledge-centre/Crime-and-social-impacts.aspx

2 Public Health England, 'The public health burden of alcohol and the effectiveness and cost-effectiveness of alcohol control policies: an evidence review', December 2016

3 https://www.bbc.co.uk/news/uk-scotland-43948081

4 Department for Transport, Drink-Drive Accidents & Casualties, 2017

III. *Possession with Intent*

5 Internal NPCC briefing, 2018 (used with permission)

6 Ellason et al. (1996), in Heffernan et al., p.797: in an inpatient substance abuse treatment setting, researchers

found a reported childhood sexual and/or physical abuse rate of 67.6 per cent (Heffernan, Karen et al (2000). Childhood Trauma as a Correlate of Lifetime Opiate Use in Psychiatric Patients. [online]. *Journal of Addictive Behaviours.* **25** (5))

7 Internal NPCC briefing, 2018 (used with permission)

8 Ibid.

9 Ibid.

10 Ibid.

IV. *Just a Domestic*

11 https://www.refuge.org.uk/our-work/forms-of-violence-and-abuse/domestic-violence/domestic-violence-the-facts/

12 HMIC, 'A progress report on the police response to domestic abuse', November 2017

13 https://www.refuge.org.uk/our-work/forms-of-violence-and-abuse/domestic-violence/domestic-violence-the-facts/

14 HMIC, 'Everyone's business: Improving the police response to domestic abuse', 2014

15 https://www.refuge.org.uk/our-work/forms-of-violence-and-abuse/domestic-violence/domestic-violence-the-facts/

16 Ibid.

17 HMIC, 'Everyone's business: Improving the police response to domestic abuse', 2014

18 https://www.theguardian.com/commentisfree/2018/oct/24/brexit-theresa-may-domestic-abuse-bill-universal-credit

19 https://www.telegraph.co.uk/politics/2019/01/10/250000-children-should-classed-victims-domestic-abuse-says-nspcc/

20 https://www.nspcc.org.uk/what-we-do/news-opinion/government-domestic-abuse-children/

V. *On a Knife Edge*

21 Public Health England, 'Introduction to Adverse Childhood Experiences', 2018

22 https://www.theguardian.com/news/2018/jul/24/violent-crime-cured-rather-than-punished-scottish-violence-reduction-unit

23 Dr Gerry Hassan, 'Violence is Preventable, not Inevitable: the Story and Impact of the Scottish Violence Reduction Unit', 2019

24 https://www.theguardian.com/cities/ng-interactive/2019/jan/14/london-killings-2018-homicides-capital-highest-decade-murders

25 https://www.thetimes.co.uk/article/tragedy-should-act-as-a-call-to-serve-our-community-lq6w82wkkor

VI. *Places of Safety*

26 Publicly available via the www.hundredfamilies.org
    website: http://www.hundredfamilies.org/wp/wp-
    content/uploads/2013/12/MARVIN_BAILEY_May11.pdf

27 HMIC, 'Policing and mental health: Picking up the
    pieces', 2018

VII. *Learning to Listen*

28 Charles Reith, *A New Study of Police History*, Oliver &
    Boyd, 1956

29 Patrick Bishop, 'When Brixton went up in Flames',
    Observer, 10 April 2011

30 https://www.bbc.co.uk/news/uk-politics-35192265

VIII. *Keeping the Peace*

31 http://news.bbc.co.uk/1/hi/england/1966826.stm

32 https://www.bbc.co.uk/sport/football/49752486

33 https://www.channel4.com/news/by/jon-snow/blogs/
    bankers-arrested

IX. *The Rise of Extremism*

34 Allport, Gordon, *The Nature of Prejudice*, Addison-
    Wesley, 1954.

35 James 3:6 New Living Translation

X. *A Question of Belief*

36 https://assets.publishing.service.gov.uk/government/
    uploads/system/uploads/attachment_data/file/214970/
    sexual-offending-overview-jan-2013.pdf

37 Home Office, 'A report by Baroness Vivien Stern CBE of
    an Independent Review into how Rape Complaints are
    handled by Public Authorities in England and Wales',
    2010, p.12

38 https://www.ons.gov.uk/releases/crimeinengland
    andwalesyearendingjune2017

39 https://www.theguardian.com/society/2019/aug/29/
    fall-in-charges-despite-rise-in-reports-is-creating-new-
    victims

40 https://www.theguardian.com/lifeandstyle/womens-
    blog/2014/nov/21/police-letting-rape-victims-down-too

41 https://www.justiceinspectorates.gov.uk/hmicfrs/our-
    work/article/rape-monitoring-group-digests/

42 https://www.bbc.co.uk/news/uk-30081682

43 https://www.theguardian.com/commentisfree/2018/
    feb/11/satanic-abuse-panic-nick-dolphin-square-
    westminster-paedophile-ring

44 https://www.xlp.org.uk/sites/default/files/documents/
    Girls-and-Gangs-FINAL-VERSION.pdf

45 https://www.theguardian.com/lifeandstyle/2008/jul/04/
    women.ukcrime

46 https://fullfact.org/news/has-one-three-teenage-girls-experienced-some-form-sexual-violence/

47 https://www.endviolenceagainstwomen.org.uk/yougov-poll-exposes-high-levels-sexual-harassment-in-schools/

48 https://www.childrenscommissioner.gov.uk/wp-content/uploads/2017/07/Basically_porn_is_everywhere.pdf

49 https://www.barnardos.org.uk/news/Police_figures_reveal_rise_of_almost_80_in_reports_of_child-on-child_sex_offences/latest-news.htm?ref=121581

50 https://www.ilo.org/global/lang--en/index.htm

51 https://www.stopthetraffik.org/arresting-people-wont-stop-human-trafficking/

XI. *On the Register*

52 https://www.gov.uk/government/publications/the-victoria-climbie-inquiry-report-of-an-inquiry-by-lord-laming

53 From the introduction to the Laming Inquiry report, p.1

54 https://thecpsu.org.uk/resource-library/research/how-safe-are-our-children-2018/

55 https://www.rotherham.gov.uk/downloads/file/1407/independent_inquiry_cse_in_rotherham

56 From the introduction to the Jay Inquiry report

57 https://www.telegraph.co.uk/women/life/telford-sex-abuse-scandal-wasnt-brave-enough-talk-race-wish/

58 https://www.iicsa.org.uk/publications/inquiry/interim

59 Matthew Syed, *Black Box Thinking*, John Murray, 2015

60 https://www.theguardian.com/society/2009/aug/16/
baby-p-family

XII. *Policing in 2020*

61 https://www.telegraph.co.uk/news/2019/08/28/falling-
rape-convictions-putting-people-risk-serial-attackers/

62 https://www.bbc.co.uk/news/uk-49459674

63 https://www.nationalcrimeagency.gov.uk/who-we-are/
publications/296-national-strategic-assessment-of-
serious-organised-crime-2019/file

64 https://assets.publishing.service.gov.uk/government/
uploads/system/uploads/attachment_data/file/817742/
hosb1119-assaults.pdf)

65 https://www.theguardian.com/politics/2006/jan/16/
conservatives.ukcrime?CMP=share_btn_link

66 https://www.standard.co.uk/news/uk/controversial-four-
horsemen-police-reformist-given-top-job-by-boris-
johnson-8138917.html

67 https://www.gov.uk/government/speeches/police-
reform-theresa-mays-speech-to-the-national-policing-
conference

68 https://www.nao.org.uk/report/financial-sustainability-
of-police-forces-in-england-and-wales-2018/

69 https://www.bbc.co.uk/news/uk-32806520

70 https://www.theguardian.com/uk-news/2018/apr/08/
police-cuts-likely-contributed-to-rise-in-violent-leaked-
report-reveals

71 https://www.parliament.uk/business/committees/
committees-a-z/commons-select/home-affairs-
committee/news-parliament-2017/policing-for-the-
future-report-published-17-19/

72 https://www.polfed.org/news-media/latest-news/2019/
government-must-face-facts-extreme-stress-in-policing-
is-real/

73 https://blogs.spectator.co.uk/2018/11/the-stop-and-
search-race-myth/

Conclusion: First and Second Things

74 Found in C. S. Lewis, *Essay Collection and Other Short Pieces*, HarperCollins, 2000

75 Michael Marmot, *The Health Gap*, Bloomsbury, 2016

76 'The economic and social costs of crime', Research Report 99

Epilogue: December 2020

77 https://www.theguardian.com/society/2020/apr/15/
domestic-abuse-killings-more-than-double-amid-covid-
19-lockdown

78 https://www.bbc.co.uk/news/uk-53498675Crime

79 https://www.bbc.co.uk/programmes/mooolwkz

80 https://learning.nspcc.org.uk/research-resources/2020/
social-isolation-risk-child-abuse-during-and-after-
coronavirus-pandemic

81 Glennon Doyle, *Untamed*, Vermillion, 2020

'A stark account of a talented police officer's breakdown...
This is a startlingly honest book and the final two chapters
are heartbreaking' *The Times*

'I read *Blue* more or less in one sitting. I thought it was wonderful
– very powerful, deeply moving and utterly honest'
Henry Marsh, bestselling author of *Do No Harm*

'This is a remarkable book... Profound and deeply moving...
It has as much to tell us about mental illness as it does
about policing' Alastair Stewart

**A searingly honest memoir of the uplifting highs and crushing
lows of a life spent policing on the front line**

John Sutherland joined the Met in 1992, having dreamed of being
a police officer since his teens. Rising quickly through the ranks,
he experienced all that is extraordinary about a life in blue: saving
lives, finding the lost, comforting the broken and helping to take
dangerous people off the streets. But for every case with a happy
ending, there were others that ended in desperate sadness, and in
2013 John suffered a major breakdown.

Blue is his memoir of crime and calamity, of adventure and
achievement, of friendship and failure, of serious illness and slow
recovery. With searing honesty, it offers an immensely moving and
personal insight into what it is to be a police officer in Britain today.